God Help Me

Finding God's Help When You Feel Hopeless

By

Carl Adam Wright

Printed in the United States of America

First Printing, 2024

ISBN 979-8-89390-042-2

Library of Congress Control Number: Pending

Ordering Information: Special discounts are available on quantity purchases by bookstores, corporations, associations, and others. For details, contact the publisher at sales@braughlerbooks.com or at 937-58-BOOKS.

For questions or comments about this book,
please write to info@braughlerbooks.com.

ACKNOWLEDGMENTS

First, I thank my Heavenly Father. I thank my wife, Allison, and my children, Lydia and Max, for their patient support. I want to thank Megan Tatreau and Elizabeth Maynard Charle for the editing work.

Table of Contents

INTRODUCTION

As I write this, it is a gloomy, rainy Monday morning. I'm on my second cup of coffee, and I'm sitting under the Amazon-controlled, golden Phillips Hue bulb. The ambiance for writing is perfect, and I feel God's presence as I describe to you where we are going in this work that you've chosen to read. I didn't really know how to begin this study, yet I truly feel compelled to write these things. It is my prayer that this work will be a help to its readers, and maybe it will serve as a catalyst for a new beginning to some. This work is meant to unapologetically point to the divine purpose of our lives. It is here we truly find peace, joy, and happiness.

I'm a simple guy. I like to keep things simple. I appreciate complex minds, but my mind is not one of them. This book will not solve the questions of the universe, and it will certainly not explain the depths of the human soul. That is far too much for me, but it will highlight two basic ways to walk through your life: aligning with God's way or wrestling against it. My purpose in this study is not to eliminate struggle from your life but to help you tap into your greatest source of peace in life's storms, of encouragement in the deepest valleys, and of managing brokenness. So, this is the point of this book: God wants to help.

I love the ocean. I love the smell of the salty air, and I love to hear the waves crashing on the shore. I love to hear seagulls begging for an unlucky crab or minnow. Growing up in the Carolinas made the beach a part of my life, and I wouldn't have it any other way.

Several years ago, I discovered the fun of kayaking in the ocean and creeks. Kayaking in the ocean has a certain art to it. There are a few things you learn quickly: Don't let the nose dip if you're riding a wave, don't forget sunscreen, and respect the ocean current and tides. I'll skip the first two hard-learned lessons and I'll save those for another time, but I do want to spend some time on the last lesson: respect the current and tides.

When I first started kayaking, I had no idea how strong the ocean current actually was. I had been in the ocean in a boat, but it was powered by something other than my arms (praise God for Johnson motors). When you are constantly fighting against the ocean, you wear out quickly. Paddling against the current makes progress slow, difficult, and exhausting. After just a few kayaking trips, I learned to check the tides before planning on going down ocean creeks. Instead of fighting the tide, I learned to let it help me. I'd go in with the tide, and if I timed it well, go out with the tide. Working with the tide makes the journey far more enjoyable.

Not too far in my past, I had an epiphany about this and the help of God (I told ya, I'm simple). I realized that if I truly believe in an almighty, loving, caring, compassionate, omnipotent God, and if I believe in his Word, I can conclude that he can help me through this journey of life. I believe his way is best, and he wants what is best for me. Therefore, I need to learn how to recognize God's way and how to let my work align with his.

I sincerely believe, with all that I am, that there is a God who loves us, intimately knows each of us, and wants to help each of us through life. We can resist his help, but life becomes so much more difficult. My toddler son loves to say, "I do it myself." I'm all for him growing, trying, and failing. I know that is good for his development, but he simply isn't strong enough to buckle his car seat. He needs help. Eventually, he will ask for help, and I gladly give it. Likewise, I believe God wants to help us with our lives.

I love to dig through my mind and explore memories. If I work at it, I can recall some remarkable details from thirty years ago. I remember my first teacher, Mrs. Porter. She was a dark-haired, pretty lady. On the floor in her classroom was a red and green rug with numbers on it. I assume it was there to help us rug rats learn to count.

One of my first field trips that I recall was to the pumpkin patch. I remember walking through a hay bale maze and each of us receiving our own small pumpkin. The memory seems so clear, and while I recall very little from that first year, the things I do remember are lodged in my memory. What I don't remember is when I developed the unhealthy fears and anxieties that have haunted my soul over the years. It seems blurry how I picked up bad mentalities and perspectives along life's way that have created so many challenges to overcome, but, like unwanted pests that find their way into our homes, those negative, dark mentalities find their way into our lives.

I've always admired those people who seem somewhat unfazed by life's pressures ... the ones who are not governed by opinions, expectations, and gossip. For me, somewhere in life, I've learned to fear the possibility of someone being disappointed. I admit it is a terrible trait, and it has haunted and taxed my soul in many ways.

I had a friend whose loud personality seemed to drown out the social anxiety of anyone around him. Admittedly, I envied that quality. For me, a crowd immediately made me want to blend. I wanted to be lost among the faces. I certainly did not want any action or sound from me to draw attention. I always dreaded those terrible moments when a teacher began the school year by going around the room, having each student state their name and something about themselves. My heart would pound, and I'd feel so nervous that I would sometimes forget my favorite color or hobby.

For me, I dreaded raising my hand because it stopped me from hiding among the crowd. I hated being called upon to answer questions. I was extremely shy and terrible at interacting with other kids. So, you can imagine that becoming a pastor, standing in front of hundreds of people was not on my radar. The five- or six-year-old version of myself would become pale at the thought of doing what I do now. Nevertheless, here I am. I must admit that all of those things from a child never really left. I just have a much different way of carrying my fears, doubts, and feelings of inadequacy.

I once heard a wonderful sermon about laying down our burdens. I remember thinking about how wonderful that sounded. Wouldn't it be nice if you could snap your fingers and feel the weight lifted? Think about everything weighing on your shoulders right now. Some burdens are external, and some burdens are internal. You may have a job you despise, a boss you cannot understand, a mortgage you barely clear each month, a troubled teenage child, a rambunctious toddler, a struggling marriage, a single parenthood, and the list could continue for days. It is not that we want these things to vanish. Some of them are interwoven with key sources of joy in our lives, but we would welcome a way to make the burdens lighter.

Then, we have our internal burdens. You may be filled with worries, insecurities, doubts, fears, painful memories, emotional scars, longings in your soul, and, again, the list could continue. If there was a way I could take my internal burdens and make them vanish, sign me up!

The problem is that many well-intended preachers and Christians along the way have led us to believe that following Jesus is about making our burdens vanish. Perhaps you've heard that, "If you are feeling heavy laden, brother or sister, just walk down this aisle and give your life to Jesus. He will make all your burdens go away!"

When I study the gospel, I find a different picture. I find a Jesus who does say, "Come to me, all who labor and are heavy laden, and I will give you rest. Take my yoke upon you, and learn from me, for I am gentle and lowly in heart, and you will find rest for your souls. For my yoke is easy, and my burden is light" (Matthew 11:28-30). But look at what Jesus is saying. Jesus never says our burdens vanish. He says that when we take his "yoke" upon us and "learn" from him, we find rest for our souls. It is hard for me not to think about eggs when I hear the word "yoke," but Jesus isn't talking about a good source of protein. He is talking about a wooden beam often used to pair oxen together. This allows the two animals to share the load. The beautiful picture Jesus gives is the load doesn't vanish, but it is shared.

All throughout the Bible, you will find God calling men and women to incredible tasks. The fears are real. The dangers are real. The burdens are real, but God also couples with those callings a promise, that he will be with them. Life's load is burdensome, but when we are united with Jesus Christ, the "burden is light." This reveals something about God's methods. He could make the burdens vanish, but he doesn't. He chooses to help us carry them. God helps us.

The words of Jesus in Matthew 11:28-30 are still true for us today. But are you ready for his help? When you are "yoked" to Jesus, you cannot walk on your own anymore. You will struggle walking in a different direction than the one you are yoked alongside.

Many people want God's help but not his direction. Many people want God's help but not his plan for their lives because they've got their own plans. Many people want God's help but not his pulling them into places of discomfort.

As we go through this study, I want to encourage you with the truth that God does want to help you, and he will help you. He will bring peace into your life that you can find nowhere else. He can truly bring your weary soul rest, but his journey might not be what you would choose.

As we begin this book, I have one question I would like you to sincerely ask yourself: Are you ready for God's help?

CHAPTER ONE

Twelve

I know that you can do all things, and that no purpose of yours can be thwarted.

— Job 42:2

Topic: We need to trust in God's power and authority.

The number twelve is a biblical number of divine authority. It is found approximately 187 times in the Bible. There were twelve sons of Jacob. There were twelve tribes of Israel. Jesus had twelve disciples. The number twelve is significant, especially when we talk about God's divine helping hand reaching into humanity. We find this number of divine authority woven into human history at times when help was desperately needed.

If we first go to the Gospel of Mark, we'll find this exact theme in the fifth chapter. Here, the woman had been bleeding for twelve years. Jesus was on his way to visit a sick twelve-year-old girl. He would soon feed the five thousand, leaving twelve baskets in excess. Each of these moments captured events when help was desperately needed, and Jesus graciously granted it through his power and authority. The message is quite clear: Jesus has divine power and authority, but there are very few people who truly trust in that power and authority. If we take an honest look at ourselves, how often do we lean on the divine power and authority of God in our own lives?

With that idea, let us continue in the Gospel of Mark. Specifically, let's look at the story from Mark 5:21-34, where Jesus encountered a woman with a hemorrhage. She had been suffering from the issue for twelve years, and for some reason, she concluded that touching the edge of Jesus's garment would heal her. Why? What made the clothing significant? It wasn't luxurious. It was a common man's garment. Its significance was in its owner. It belonged to Jesus.

Whatever belongs to Jesus immediately becomes significant. A dusty, common piece of clothing has little value, but put Jesus in it, and the story changes. The same is true with life. Without Jesus, life is meaningless. It is empty. We go from one well to the other, drinking only to thirst again. Put Jesus into that life, and there is value and eternal significance.

This woman with the hemorrhage, in the Gospel of Mark, saw that the world had nothing to fix her feeling of brokenness. For twelve years, the woman had found no solution no matter where she turned. She had visited a number of physicians and depleted her life's savings. She was desperate for a solution, and then she heard of this man named Jesus. Though there were many differing opinions of Jesus, his power to heal wasn't really disputed, even among his enemies. This woman saw Jesus as one who had power and authority over what had kept her broken, outcast, and empty.

Is that true of you? Do you truly believe that Jesus has power and authority over all the stuff in your life? There are so many people who claim to have faith, but they have so little trust in God. Faith has become a term we associate with religious gatherings, but what do we really believe about Jesus?

This woman struggled through the thick mob that had gathered around Jesus. Stumbling and prying through the shuffling bodies, she found her way to the famous Jesus. She reached out with all her strength to grab just the edge of his garment. I picture a scene where the mob was "thronged about him," (Mark 5:24) and, with her arm fully extended and her fingers stretched, she reached. The kicked-up dust made visibility difficult, but on her hands and knees, she continued pressing toward the edge of this carpenter's robe. Finally, her persistence and reach accomplished the mission as she gripped the fringe of his garment.

There is another piece to the story that should not be overlooked: the healing was beyond the woman's ability, but her persistence remained. She did not stop reaching and trying to get to Jesus. The great temptation was to stop persisting and reaching, but all challenges require some level of persistence. We must not stop pursuing what is within our reach.

The gospel account says, "Immediately," she was healed. For twelve years, all hope seemed lost, but when she touched *his* garment, her life was changed. This was a miracle of Jesus, and miracles are not the normal way of the natural world. But, the help of God is present in the natural world all the time. It is accessed by faith.

Many people claim to live by "faith," but I'm not sure many of us appreciate the gravity of that word. Faith is more than a description of whether or not you believe in God. Faith is transformative in how you think.

According to the National Institute of Mental Health (NIMH), 19.1 percent of U.S. adults have some anxiety disorder.[1] The American Psychiatric Association (APA) did a study in 2022 that recorded 83 percent of U.S. adults were stressed about inflation, and 57 percent indicated that money was a significant source of stress in their lives.[2] I personally struggle with General Anxiety Disorder (GAD) and Major Depressive Disorder (MDD). While the physiological issue needs treatment, there is a spiritual mentality that can help us combat diseases of the mind.

---

[1] https://www.nimh.nih.gov/health/statistics/any-anxiety-disorder

[2] https://www.apa.org/news/press/releases/stress/2022/concerned-future-inflation

When I submerge myself in the truth, the lies of the mind have accountability. With my GAD, I often believe the worst of nearly every situation is unavoidable when, in reality, the situation is rarely as bad as my mind leads me to believe. With my MDD, I often feel that my life is overshadowed by darkness, but the reality is that God has blessed me with many wonderful things. Again, my mind operates in a cloud of deception. That deception is real, but the lies produced in my mind are not real. So when I truly believe there is a God who loves me, and he sent his Son to be a sacrifice for my wrongdoing, my mind has to contend with a good, eternal status, though my depression brings temporary pain.

The woman in Mark 5 had a long-term struggle, but she also had come to believe in a long-term solution. Though the pain of her situation was present when she desperately fought to get close to Jesus, there was hope and trust in her heart that her situation was temporary. For many of us, we need to fix our hearts upon the truth of Jesus and the truth of eternity with him. Our present problem does not have eternal power, but we serve a God who does.

Let the truth minimize the power of the lies in your mind. If you are in Jesus, you have hope and a future!

Dr. Mary Neal, the author of *7 Lessons from Heaven: How Dying Taught Me to Live a Joy-Filled Life*, wrote of her near-death experience (NDE) that brought her into a deep, genuine relationship with Jesus Christ. I want to credit her with a phrase from that book that I'd never really heard before reading her work. The phrase is: "transformational trust."

Dr. Neal shared that her face-to-face encounter with death and our creator taught her that God loves and cares for each one of us deeply. She expressed how her experience brought her from a cultural Christianity to a transformational trust in Jesus Christ. I love her wording because there are many of us out there in the world today who really need to change our thinking. We cannot continue to have a Sunday morning faith when we face a life of difficulty seven days a week. We need a trust that changes how we see our fears, struggles, and even sin.

The woman with the issue of bleeding in Mark 5 displayed a powerful, life-altering trust in the power of Jesus. The moment she felt her healing through his power marked a moment of transformation in her life. She would never be the same.

It is also interesting that there were so many people around Jesus who touched him, but they did not share the same experience as the woman. In Mark 5:31, Jesus recognized that the faith of the woman brought his power upon her, and he asked, "Who touched me?" The disciples, who seemed puzzled by the question, commented, "You see the crowd pressing around you..." The implication was people were bumping into Jesus left and right, but only one experienced transformation. Surely, the mob of people was filled with problems. Maybe not all of them are physical, but every individual there that day needed some form of healing, yet we read of only one who received it.

The faith of the woman in Mark 5:21-34 was unique. She truly believed that Jesus radiated a power so profound his garment was enough to fix what her life savings could not. Perhaps there was desperation in her attempt, but her faith was sincere. It was a "transformational trust."

That's exactly the attitude we need in facing our issues as well. If we really believe in the perfect goodness and greatness of God coupled with omnipotence, then we should face each day with trust. God has your struggle in his hand. The struggle doesn't hold you; God holds the struggle. In God's hands the woman's issue of blood became a testimony written in the Word of God to be shared for thousands of years as Jesus's power over our issues.

Another example of God's power and authority through the number twelve is in the Old Testament. The story is found in Exodus 15:22-27. Moses was leading the people of Israel out of Egypt, but they ran out of water. The people of Israel arrived at a place called "Marah," which means bitterness. Not only was the water too bitter to drink, but the attitude of Israel had turned bitter toward Moses and God. It was here that Moses cried out in desperation to God for help, and God helped Moses. God told Moses to toss a log into the water, and the water became sweet instead of bitter. The people saw that God's hand can turn that which is bitter and sweet. Immediately following this miracle, God led the people to Elam, "where there were twelve springs of water and seventy palm trees, and they encamped there by the water." Once again, people who found themselves struggling witnessed the power and authority of God over their predicament.

Without water, Israel's journey in the wilderness would have been short-lived, yet when things got bitter, Moses asked God to make it better. There is a valuable truth in this situation. God left a gap between what Israel could understand and the larger plan he was unfolding. The gap could not be crossed by logic or sight, but it was faith in his divine authority and power. They did not get to the "twelve" springs until they experienced the bitterness of Marah and the blessing of watching him work.

One of the patterns surrounding the number twelve in these scriptural accounts is God's action following our trust. We naturally assume the reverse is how trust is built. Typically, trust is slowly earned, quickly broken, and rarely issued. The problem is that we miss the difference between trusting a holy, righteous, omniscient, and omnipotent God and a sinful, flawed human being. God continually reminds us as his people that we can trust him to not only take care of us but to lead us in the best possible paths for our lives.

The story of Israel arriving at the twelve springs and seventy palms of Elim is sandwiched between cycles of God helping Israel and Israel, quickly forgetting how lovingly God had cared for them and led them. God was teaching Israel that they could trust him in all things because he had power over all things: nations conquered, nature surrendered, and needs were met all through his power and authority.

The constant need for people to be reminded of God's power would surface again under Joshua's leadership in Joshua 4. God tells Joshua to, "Take twelve men from the people, from each tribe a man, and command them, saying, 'Take twelve stones from here out of the midst of the Jordan, from the very place where the priests' feet stood firmly.'" The twelve stones would serve as a reminder that God stopped the Jordan River so the people of Israel could cross into the land God had promised. It was his authority and power that made a way for the Israelites to enjoy freedom from the bondage of Egypt in a land where they belonged. It was a reminder that God has the power and authority to take care of his people no matter what stands in the way.

The story in Joshua 4 gives us a practical takeaway for how we can experience the help of God. We can simply be reminded of all we have come through. I encourage you to find something that is a physical reminder of the spiritual journey God has brought you through. In Joshua 4, the twelve stones were a reminder that God made a way to enter the land he had promised. He stopped the Jordan River. What has God done for you in the past that reminds you to trust him in the present and future? Set up a physical reminder you can look at or take with you that helps you fight doubts and fears. Remember what God has done, and he has the power and authority to do it again.

Let us do a brief recap on what this chapter is really about. Twelve is the biblical number of divine authority, and the Bible is saturated with examples of God's power and authority helping people overcome what they could not do on their own. God has helped his people throughout history, but it is through the avenue of faith.

Let me pause here and make a distinction between genuine trust and attempting to please God through an act of faith. Faith in all of these encounters with God was not saying, "God, if I just have enough faith, you'll come through for me." That is a satanic lie and a misinterpretation of Jesus's teaching on faith that can move mountains. God does not remove every thorn as the apostle Paul discovered, a man of great faith. When we have that transformational trust in God's divine authority and power, we are saying, "God, you know what is best for me, and I am trusting your divine authority with my life. I know that I can trust you to help me with whatever I face, and you want to help me, not harm me. I trust you however you see fit to help. Your way is what I trust."

So, the real question to ask yourself at this point is: Do I believe in Jesus's divine authority and power? If the answer is a sincere "yes," then you need to follow that answer with another question: Do you believe God is good? Do you believe he really loves and cares for each and every soul? If the answer is still yes for each question, then you are ready to do something transformational in your life. Trust him with whatever it is that has you so concerned. With a sincere heart, trust him and ask him to help you, expecting that he will. Trust him.

Reflection:

1. Does your trust in God change the way you live your life?
2. Do you believe God has authority over the things in your life that scare you the most?
3. Is there an ongoing issue stealing joy from your life?
4. What spiritual steps have you taken to experience a transformational trust in Jesus?

CHAPTER TWO

Helplessness to Hopelessness

I am the vine; you are the branches. Whoever abides in me and I in him, he it is that bears much fruit, for apart from me you can do nothing.

— John 15:5

Topic: God wants to help us.

When I was in college, I dated a girl at another university not far from my school. It was about a forty-five-minute commute. As I drove down the Interstate, I noticed the interior dash lights in my car had suddenly stopped working. The sun was low in the evening sky, and I could not see my speedometer or any gauges. I became concerned about my headlights possibly not working either. So, I pulled into a Walmart parking lot and opened the hood. I looked underneath as an eighteen-year-old boy, clueless as to what I was doing.

I began reading through the manual. I checked all the fuses and plugs. Nothing worked. I wasn't that nervous for the first hour, but when I quickly narrowed all my options, the picture became more and more desperate. Not to mention, there were many things going on underneath the surface.

I felt broken. I felt that everything in my life was failing. I was running from God, running from my calling (more about this later). I had problems with my roommate. I felt disconnected. I was far from home and I was broke. While all these things seem like water under the bridge now, when I was younger, and in the moment, it was overwhelming.

I walked into Walmart, and I met the employee behind the counter in the automotive section. I told him my truck had broken down and I needed help. The man behind the counter looked at me with a puzzled look on his face and snapped, "There's all this stuff we have over there." I was discouraged. I wanted him to say, "Sure, we can help you," even if not really all that sincere. Just the words would have helped. I wanted him to ask what was wrong. I wanted him to help me diagnose the problem. Instead, I received a cold shoulder, and there was no help. It became clear I was on my own, or at least I thought so.

I bought a few tools I probably didn't need, but it made me feel better, and I returned to my truck. I remember disconnecting the battery and some other things (I'm not sure what they were). Then I stopped, and I just sat down in the parking lot and leaned against my truck. I prayed with deep sincerity from my place of hopelessness, "God, help me."

About that time, a dark-colored BMW pulled up beside my truck. Inside the vehicle was a very kind woman. She looked at me with a compassionate expression on her face, and she said, "Are you okay?" I wanted to shout, "No, ma'am! I am falling apart faster than my truck!" But I responded politely rather than honestly, "Thank you, but I'm just taking a break." The lady looked at me as though she knew I was lying. Then she said something that caught me off guard. "It is all going to work out," she said, smiling. Her kindness and positivity were such a comfort in that moment.

I have never seen this lady again, and I don't know who this lady was. But I felt she was an answer to my prayer. I had cried out to God, "Help me!" He did.

I calmed down. I reconnected the battery, and I climbed into my truck. Suddenly, I noticed a dial I had not noticed before. I ran my finger across the dial, and my lights started working. Feeling like a complete idiot, I started my truck. All along, things were okay. Besides being at a point in my life where I learned I needed to know more about cars, I also learned a bit about God's helping hand.

In the day-to-day spiritual journey, we have the ultimate Helper. He is real, and he is present. Not only is God with us, but he wants to help us. Scripture teaches us that God is good (Psalm 145:9). Jesus taught that we are to call on him as our Father in Heaven. So, if we have a good Father in Heaven, what does that mean for us? How does a good father treat his children?

A good father loves his children. He cares about their needs, and he cares about their struggles. I'm far from a perfect father, but I care deeply for my children. When I hear them cry, I want to rush to their aid. I want to help them in any way I can. If I, an imperfect, sinful man, care for the needs of my children, I can only begin to imagine how much a perfect God cares for his children. Therefore, we have great news. God is our good, heavenly father. He loves us, and we can rest assured that his helping hand is present. Look at what Jesus told us in the Sermon on the Mount (Matthew 7:11): "If you then, who are evil, know how to give good gifts to your children, how much more will your Father who is in heaven give good things to those who ask him!"

Unfortunately, the blindness of the physical world to the spiritual realities is always a struggle for those of us on this side of eternity. From that struggle, we can feel so distant from a God who is so close. We can lose sight of the eternal shaping that is taking place, and the temporary, physical world becomes discouraging. British evangelist G. Campbell Morgan said: "Our distance from God is that of inability to know and apprehend the near. It is the distance of the blind man from the glory of the picture in front of him. The distance of the deaf man from the beauty of the symphony sounding round about him. It is the distance of the sensate man from all the movement of life in the midst of which he lives." The trials become overwhelming. We can feel like we don't know what to do or who to turn to for help.

Many times we feel like we are on our own and like we have to figure it all out ourselves. I believe some of the four most painful words we can receive are: I can't help you. Personally, saying this phrase to someone is painful, and receiving this phrase brings a feeling of hopelessness.

If you have ever found yourself in a place of helplessness, the last phrase on the planet you want to hear from someone else is, "I can't help you."

Helplessness quickly evolves into hopelessness. Hopelessness is a feeling that will steal from you an ability to enjoy the life God has given you. If you are feeling helpless, it is my prayer for you that you know the fight is not yours alone. You may feel alone, and God may feel distant. Both are untrue.

We all go through different things, but many of us have probably, at some time or another, said, "God, help me." Perhaps, for some, it wasn't meant to be a sincere cry for help as much as it was an expression, but I believe those three words make up one of the most powerful prayers we can pray. The problem most of us have is we really don't believe God cares enough, listens enough, or is involved enough to actually help.

We could not be more wrong if that is our line of thinking. God wants to help, and he will help.

It is a hazard to our spiritual health to adopt the idea that God doesn't care about our situations. When we start believing this lie, we start disconnecting from God. We stop calling out to him about "the little things." This should be a warning light.

I recently read about the world's most deadly creature to human beings. You may think, like me, that the deadliest must be the scariest. My mind immediately shifted to some kind of snake or ferocious lion. I pictured the man-crushing jaws of a crocodile. However, the deadliest creature to humans on earth is the mosquito. It is responsible for over 700,000 deaths per year.[3]

The mosquito, at first thought, seems like an unlikely candidate. As a country boy from South Carolina, I've had my share of "skeeter" bites, but I've never considered the dangers of the tiny pests. They carry tons of diseases, and in various places in the world, those diseases will send you to an early grave.

Much like the mosquito, our little disconnects with God may not seem like a big deal, but the dangers of the perspective should not be overlooked. When we stop turning to God with our problems, we are

---

[3] Jeremiah, David. *God Has Not Forgotten You.*

inevitably turning to something else. We start shifting our faith and our focus. The book of Hebrews tells us, [6] "And without faith, it is impossible to please him, for whoever would draw near to God must believe that he exists and that he rewards those who seek him" (Hebrews 11:6). Why is it that we will share our problems with a close friend but not with God? Why is it that we will Google problems and concerns before we lay them at the feet of our Lord, Jesus?

I encourage you today to go to the Lord with any of your concerns. God can and will help you. Now, God's way of helping may not align with your desired form of help, which we will discuss later in the book, but I know my Heavenly Father. I know he loves us so deeply that we cannot begin to fathom such depth. Consider the words of the prophet Isaiah (Isaiah 41:10): "Fear not, for I am with you; be not dismayed, for I am your God; I will strengthen you, I will help you, I will uphold you with my righteous right hand."

I'm no biblical scholar, but the verse above does not seem to give the impression that God doesn't care about the problems of his people. As we study the Bible, we consistently find God concerned for his people. He wants to be a part of their lives, connecting with them on a personal level.

In this book, we will zoom in on a man who seemed to have a unique connection and understanding of God's divine help and strength. He is the only man in biblical history to carry the title of "a man after God's own heart." He had experiences he endured that linked him to many of our stories, yet he never stopped leaning into God's help. He knew what it was like to be homeless, and he knew what it was like to be betrayed. He knew what it was like to be captivated by lust and commit adultery. He knew what it was like to lose a baby. He knew what it was like to lose a grown son. Through all of these valleys, he never found himself without God's help and presence. His name was David, and as we look at some critical points in his life, I pray that God's Word reveals something to you.

It is my prayer that this look at David's life will speak to someone looking for help, and just like David realized, our greatest source of help and strength is God Almighty. I want to ask that you read this book with an open heart and mind to some biblical ways of thinking that may have a dramatic impact on your circumstances. A deep trust in God's providence changes the way we see our struggles. In Isaiah 26:3, we see the effects of trusting God: "You keep him in perfect peace whose mind is stayed on you because he trusts in you." So, let us go forward together in a way to connects our greatest struggles to our greatest Helper.

Reflection:

1. Would you consider your current life circumstances hopeless?

2. Trace the pathway of your biggest struggle back in your mind before it was a struggle. What changed in your life that led you to where you are now? How much have you involved God?

3. What is your number one source of assistance you turn to for help?

4. Are you willing to make dramatic changes to see God's helping hand work in your life? If so, what needs to change?

CHAPTER THREE
Where Does My Help Come From?

"I lift up my eyes to the hills.

From where does my help come?

My help comes from the LORD,

who made heaven and earth."

— Psalm 121:1-2

Topic: To connect with God, we need to interact with him.

There was a young man once, who became famous in his land. When he was just a teenager, he became a military hero. He was invited to dine with the king of his land. Crowds cheered his name. He wasn't from an impressively wealthy family, but his fortunes in life seemed to be heading to greatness. One day, the young man accomplished a seemingly impossible feat for the king, and the king announced to the entire land that he would give his daughter's hand in marriage to this brave, young warrior.

Life seemed to be going great! A teenage hero from the middle of nowhere married into the royal family—he was living the dream, but there was a dark side to the bright future. The king was secretly jealous of the young boy. His goal in asking the impossible of the young lad was to see him fail. The king secretly wanted him dead. He never really expected to see him marry his daughter. Now, the king could not go back on his word, and the popularity of the young man was unmatched. The king could not outright kill this beloved boy. No. It had to be done in secret, or he would have to first destroy the boy's reputation.

One night, the king sat by the fire in his private quarters. He watched the embers glow while the anger in his heart burned even hotter. "The people love this pathetic worm. They cheer his name, but what about me? What about their king! Now, he sleeps with my daughter as her husband. I'll not stand for it! I'll have his head. I will have his name be banished from this land!"

The king devised an evil plot. He decided he would send a small group of faithful soldiers to eliminate the boy at his home. It would be quick and silent, and he could write a phony story to appease the people who were faithful to the boy.

The date of the attack was set. He had informed his close guards to keep watch on the boy's home. "When he comes out of his home early in the morning, strike him dead!" said the king as his parting instruction to the assassins. The men were loyal to the king, and their captain nodded at the king's order as though he was giving his seal of approval. It was done. The boy's life would now come to a bloody end, or so the king thought.

The king's daughter went to her father's home for a visit, but she saw trusted soldiers gathered around her father. She eased closer to the group without being spotted. As her father's rage steamed, his tone grew louder, and his plot to kill her husband carried loud enough to give her certainty: her husband's life was in danger. She quickly departed without being spotted and ran home.

"You must flee before nightfall! I've heard my father, and he intends to end your life by morning. The army commanders support my father, and so will their men. You must get out of here and hide until it is safe." She spoke with tears in her eyes.

"I'll go, but what about my family? What about you? How long must I go into hiding? Where will I go?" Suddenly, they heard a sound down the hall. There were no more words spoken. They kissed each other. The young man grabbed a cloak and quickly ran out the back door.

Tears ran down his face as worry consumed his thoughts. His life in luxury was about to change. For quite some time, he would be on the run and in hiding.

The young man's name was David, and the story is based on scripture's account of what happened after David married Michal. In moments, David's life was quickly turned upside down, but isn't that how it happens to us?

Life circumstances can change so fast. A doctor says, "You have cancer." Suddenly, everything changes. A spouse says, "I'm leaving." In the blink of an eye, your world dismantles. You receive a phone call, and a voice on the other end says, "There has been an accident."

These moments alter life completely. All of the stability we thought we had is gone like the wind. On the axis of dramatic change, we find the clearest, though painful, perspective on life. Life is filled with uncertainty clothed in a false sense of stability. We are, like David, always one moment from a vastly different set of circumstances.

How did David make it through the avalanche of life's normal circumstances? How did David become closer to God instead of becoming bitter? How did David go on to experience joyous days?

God's Word is true, and believing it is true sparks an immediate revelation: God loves us and is with us. Sometimes, people who claim Christianity become experts in using phrases or terminology that don't mean anything deep in their hearts. God wants us to do as the Psalmist (119:11) says, "I have stored up your words in my heart that I might not sin against you." When we adopt something as truth in our hearts, those words become a passion. We cling to those concepts as pathways by which we take steps in our lives toward a purpose. Note the contrast between closing your eyes and speaking some words into the air and closing your eyes and seeing Jesus before you, talking to him in conversation, seeing his inspired word as a "lamp to your feet" in a world of darkness.

In a sermon by Charles H. Spurgeon in the 1850s, he preached that the lofty oration of prayer we lift in Sunday morning church (if not sincere) might be as meaningless as a Pharisee prayer, but the cry of a blind beggar, Bartimaeus, "O Son of David! Have mercy on me," went straight to the ear of Jesus. Jesus then stopped and healed Bartimaeus. The passionate cry from the soul is what truly connects to God. When was the last passionate cry from your soul that the Lord heard?

The point is simple: If we want a real connection with God, we need a real conversation with him. To do that, we need to have more than an introduction to God. We need to have interaction.

David interacted with God all the time. As a result, he became familiar with God's attributes. He knew God was loving. He knew God was faithful. He knew his wrath. While David could never understand the mind of God, he could know God's desire for his life.

This helped David align with God's path for his life, and he could trust that path was best, even when it did not appear to be so.

Now, I believe there are a lot of people who would love to interact with God, but there is simply the question: How? How do we interact with a being whom we cannot see and (in most cases) hear? The answer is to start with the tangible Word to understand the ways of the intangible God.

The Word of God is always the place we should start when it comes to getting to know God. We live in the digital age, and I certainly appreciate many parts of it. For a moment, though, let's roll back the clock a couple hundred years. How would you communicate with a relative who lived in a distant country? You would write a letter. That is exactly what the Bible is—a letter to humanity from God. The unique nature of the Bible is that it was written by about forty different men over the span of approximately 1600 years, but all these men felt the inspiration of a holy God and wrote a consistent message to mankind from God. The letter reveals many things about its author, and this is how we begin to interact. We study what God has revealed in his letter about himself.

The letter (the Bible) tells us what God likes and what he doesn't like. It tells us why he created us. It tells us that he loves us. It tells us that we must be careful because we also have a spiritual enemy that lures us away from our loving God. The Bible also tells us that God isn't a distant figure, but he chooses to be woven into our lives. He develops intricate plans for us, and he gifts us the ability to choose to follow his plans or to choose our own ways.

The Bible is the starting point that gives us a real picture of who God is, but another vastly important part of interacting with God is the Holy Spirit of God. Unlike the Bible (our letter from God), the Holy Spirit cannot be seen, but the Holy Spirit is God. The Holy Spirit can be felt, but it is in a far deeper way than our physical or emotional senses.

I've learned to deeply love and enjoy time with my Bible and the Holy Spirit. I am telling you, friend, that there is deep peace, amazing joy, and unbelievable comfort in taking time away from everything else in your life to spend in the Bible with an awareness of the Holy Spirit.

Jesus shared in John 16:7-11:

Nevertheless, I tell you the truth: it is to your advantage that I go away, for if I do not go away, the Helper will not come to you. But if I go, I will send him to you. And when he comes, he will convict the world concerning sin and righteousness and judgment: concerning sin, because they do not believe in me; concerning righteousness, because I go to the Father, and you will see me no longer; concerning judgment, because the ruler of this world is judged.

In this passage, Jesus described the advantage of the "Helper," that is, the Holy Spirit. God not only wants to help you in life, but his Spirit walks with you. Let's not get lost here in too deep of a concept because there is something practical you do not want to miss. When the Spirit of God is with you, you have divine guidance.

The Helper will prompt you with little feelings in everyday life. I was with my wife one night on a date. We had driven down to one of the closest cities to us, and we were in traffic on our way to dinner. I was sitting at a red light when, all of a sudden I felt a clear prompting to change lanes. It made little sense to me because the traffic was just as bad in the lane beside me. Nevertheless, I changed lanes. Moments later, we could hear the roar of an engine in the distance, but it rapidly approached. I looked beside me just in time to see the car next to me get rear-ended by a couple of thieves on the run from the police. The car slid into the intersection, and police cars quickly surrounded the vehicle at fault. Police jumped out of their cars with weapons drawn. I felt like I was living in a movie scene.

On the way home, my wife, Allison, and I kept talking about how crazy the timing of our getting out of that lane was. We were glad the other car's passengers were okay, but we were also glad we avoided the accident. I kept thinking: Why did I change lanes? Now, as I have grown in my faith, I'm certain that was the Helper that Jesus told us about in John.

This is certainly not saying that God will always guide you out of car crashes or some other painful occurrence, but this is to say that the Helper does prompt us. He does guide us. He does prompt us to make decisions that will be best for our good and his glory.

Do not ignore those "gut feelings." Explore them. Find out why you feel you should or shouldn't do something. Do not go out on a date with that guy whom you "Just have a bad feeling about." First, find out why that feeling is there. He may be a good guy, and God just wants you to know something first, but he may be on a bad path for you. Just remember God wants what is best for you. He has sent his one and only son to make a way for you to reconnect with him, and he left his Holy Spirit to help us. We need to approach our lives with attentive souls. Blessed are those who listen.

God also wants intimacy in our interactions. We often speak to God as though we don't really care about how he feels. We've often launched quick, insincere phrases to Heaven to check our box for our daily prayer time. For some of us, God hears from us mostly when we say a blessing before a meal. Then, we often grumble at God because we feel disconnected from him when life turns in a bad direction.

We make our prayers sound good and "appropriate." I have never been more uncomfortable with a prayer than when I was a part of an event in which my close friend delivered an opening prayer. He submitted his prayer prior to the event "for approval or changes." During the event, the "approved" prayer was read by my friend. To this day, I have been bothered by this occurrence.

I have a great love and respect for my friends who shared in that event, but I could not disagree more with an approach to God. God wants authenticity. God wants the soul to speak. If you truly want God to listen to you, speak to him from the depths of your soul. God wants an intimacy with you.

The Bible gives you a promise in James 4:8, "Draw near to God, and he will draw near to you." I can give testimony to the beautiful truth of this verse. God stands with open arms to us all, but we must "draw near to him." When we do, we experience what it means to feel the presence of God in our lives. We feel his prompting, and we can rest in his strength. We feel his love, and we feel his faithful helping hand.

Reflection:

1. How would you describe your alone time with God?
2. How often in the past six months have you spent time alone with God?
3. Would you consider the amount of time you spend in close connection with God healthy?
4. Where can you carve out time to spend with God, if only for a few minutes a day?
5. How is your prayer life? Are your prayers deeply drawn from the well of your soul, or are they skimming the surface of your life, hurried and routine?

CHAPTER FOUR
Exhausted Options

I love you, O Lord, my strength.

The Lord is my rock and my fortress and my deliverer,

my God, my rock, in whom I take refuge,

my shield, and the horn of my salvation, my stronghold.

I call upon the Lord, who is worthy to be praised,

and I am saved from my enemies.

— Psalm 18:1-3

Topic: Struggles help our faith grow.

Immediately after David escaped Saul's trap, he headed a couple miles outside of Jerusalem to a place called Nob. Stressed and sweaty, his appearance was disheveled, but David was tough and smart. He knew a priest at the tabernacle, which was in Nob, and he met with him.

Ahimelech, the priest, greeted David but was suspicious that David wasn't being entirely truthful. Nevertheless, Ahimelech gave David some holy bread, and just as David was about to head on his way, he spotted Doeg the Edomite, Saul's chief herdsman. Doeg was bad news, and David must have sensed it because he followed with one more question of Ahimelech. He asked if he had any weapons, and Ahimelech shared with David that there was only one weapon available. It was the sword of Goliath, the giant David killed. David quickly accepted by stating, "There are none like it."

Now, on the surface, this story doesn't seem like a big ordeal, but put yourself in David's shoes. He has left everything behind. He has no place to go. The king of his land, his father-in-law, wants him dead. He doesn't have time to connect with his family. He leaves his home without a plan or idea of what to do.

In 1 Samuel 21 (which I have summarized), David gathered whatever supplies he could to make haste to safety. David was desperate because he had nearly exhausted his options.

When David took the sword of Goliath and said, "There are none like it," he wasn't talking about its beauty or design. Sure, maybe it was unique in appearance compared to the average sword, but David's words were more about what it meant to him. There was no other sword that represented the victory over the giant that couldn't be killed. There was no other sword that could give him the comfort and hope that this sword could. This sword was a message to David's soul from his Almighty God. That message was that God had been with him in dire circumstances before this, and he was with him now.

God rarely pulls people out of bad circumstances; rather, he comforts us by inserting himself into them with us. If you read David's Psalms, specifically Psalm 4:1 (NLT), "Answer me when I call to you, O God who declares me innocent. Free me from my troubles. Have mercy on me and hear my prayer." It is obvious that David, like many of us, would prefer God provide an instant escape from his problems. After all, he was talking to the creator of the universe. He was completely capable of making things immediately change for David, yet God chose to help David in a different way. He gave David a reminder.

When David held Goliath's sword in his hand, I imagine he flashed back to the field of battle that day. He remembered Goliath's mockery. He remembered the lack of support from his brothers. He remembered the giggles of the veteran soldiers.

He also remembered God's presence. He remembered that God let him face the giant and carry the sling, but he remembered God's strength and help. He remembered that Goliath fell.

God helped David that day at Nob by reminding him of his presence and his plan. Many times, we cry out for help from God, and we expect him to operate only in the miraculous, quick-fix way. My wife was once trying to calm my daughter, who was four at the time, and my wife asked my daughter to pray to help her calm down. "Honey, pray and ask God to help you calm down." Lydia, my daughter, responded, "It doesn't work, Momma! It doesn't work. I've tried it before."

I believe there are many people who feel this way. They do not pray because they have prayed, and God didn't speak from Heaven. God didn't immediately heal their sickness. God didn't immediately stop the pain of their circumstances. As a result, their heart also cries, "It doesn't work!"

Sometimes, God helps through miracles, but there is a bigger picture to consider. You are not who you used to be. You are stronger. You are tougher. With every challenge and with every battle, you are becoming something greater than you were in your past. When we cry out to God for help, expecting immediate rescue, we are asking God to remove a key part of growth and development in our lives.

Have you ever wondered why Jesus allowed the disciples to face storms on the Sea of Galilee, especially when he was in the boat with them? One of my favorite Bible stories is found in Luke 8:22-25. The disciples got in the boat with Jesus, and he said, "Let us go across to the other side of the lake." While following Jesus's command and direction, a storm arose. The best part was that Jesus had fallen asleep. The boat was in danger of sinking, and they screamed at Jesus, "Master, we are perishing!" It wasn't until then that Jesus calmed the storm. Why? Perhaps it was that the disciples needed to experience the storm and God's power over it. I think we can argue that the disciples gained something far greater from watching God calm the storm than if they had never been through one.

There was a moment in my life when I questioned the authority of scripture. I asked myself, sincerely, what do I really believe? Perhaps the greatest source of struggle for my faith was: Why does suffering exist if God is sovereign? I truly wrestled with this question. I came to a crossroads of who I was. I decided to trust what I could not understand. There are many apologists who have great answers to some of these questions, but ultimately, there comes a moment when we arrive at the place of embrace with finite humanity and infinite divinity. It is a place of trust where we say, "God, I trust that in your hands I can confidently rest."

The pain of surgery may make us question the surgeon and the process. However, we have come to know that a painful surgery can produce a positive result. We are eternal creatures trapped in temporary flesh. If I believed this world was all there was, I don't believe I could accept the concept of a good God. The world is filled with such horror, injustice, terrible disease, and unjust war. If this was the extent of creation from the creator, it would seem like torture with no purpose. However, this is not what the Bible teaches. We are taught that this world is quickly fading. "For God so loved the world that he sent his only son that whoever believes in him would not perish but have eternal life." God wants to save us from the sinking ship because we are far from the intended shore.

So when I trust the Bible's teaching of a good, faithful, loving God, I can be confident that even in the darkness of this life, God has good ahead. When David struggled at Nob with a difficult and uncertain season in his life, the sword of Goliath reminded him of God's helping hand. God cared for David. God loved David, and God had good for David "in the land of the living" and in eternity. Rest assured of the consistent nature of God (Malachi 3:6). Those things are true for you, too.

Sometimes, God gives us the Goliath battles to look back on for Goliath-sized hope. When the next difficult circumstance comes, we may have a memory, not a miracle, but it provides comfort and peace, helping us learn to trust God and His way of doing things.

Perhaps you have been praying for help, but you do not feel like it's working. I want to encourage you to think back through your life about some struggles and how far you've come. Those struggles have helped shape you for what you're facing now. Just like David, you can look back on those Goliath battles, and you can see how God has helped you this far. You can see how you made it here against all odds, logic, and expectation. Hang in there! There is a helping hand at work.

Reflection:

1. Do you feel like you're running out of places to turn in your life?
2. Is God giving you symbols of encouragement?
3. Have you thought back about the times God has brought you through?
4. Take a moment to feel peace and comfort in God's promises despite your circumstances.

CHAPTER FIVE
Changing Perspective

"Be not like a horse or a mule, without understanding,

which must be curbed with bit and bridle,

or it will not stay near you."

— Psalm 32:9

Topic: God helps us through suffering.

I'm convinced that suffering teaches the most powerful lessons. We often never forget the pain. I'm not saying that God only helps us through painful circumstances, but I am saying that the help of God is far more complex than positive experiences.

God's help does not always look the way we want it to look. Not every painful experience is understandable, and we do not always see a good purpose in it. Sometimes, the pain in the moment is nearly unbearable. Sometimes, the loss is inconceivable as a good thing, but right beside us is a good God who loves us. He hears our cries for help. He knows our innermost feelings. The pain is real, but so is the God who loves you. That good God gives us a great promise in Romans 8:28, "And we know that for those who love God all things work together for good, for those who are called according to his purpose."

Now, before I go any further, let me state that the purpose of this book is not an apologetic argument. There are far more capable people out there to help you work to a place of evidence for the God of the Bible. I do, however, want to make a case for a deeply connected God. The Bible clearly depicts God as one who cares about every person and their lives. Our Lord Jesus said, "…even the hairs of your head are all numbered." (Luke 12:7) I think there is an overwhelmingly large group of people who believe there is a higher power out there, but they do not believe he cares or has an interest in our affairs. While I'm not certain of all the reasons many people have adopted the idea of a disconnected god, one reason seems clear: many people perceive that God's helping hand is missing in their own struggles.

But what if God's help doesn't always look like help? What if some of the hard days are God's helping days? What if the path of least resistance isn't what is best for developing you into who God wants you to become? In the next few paragraphs, we'll look at a few steps for recognizing God's helping hand in the middle of our chaotic, challenging lives.

As we journey briefly through how God can use suffering to help, I want to be sure you do not feel like I'm saying that your suffering is good. God can use it for good, but suffering was not part of the plan for us. God protected humanity from suffering in the Garden of Eden. Temptation and sin bring suffering, and it is always tragic. It is painful, and many things you have been through were awful. I would never belittle what you have been through, but I want to explore how God can help us even through bad things.

First, if we want to know about God's help in our lives, we need to adjust our perspectives. Let's look at how to recognize God's helping hand, especially when things look dim. God has been helping people since the beginning of time, but God's help doesn't fit our standards. We think God's timing is bad, his pathway too difficult, and his process too messy, yet I see in my own life how those moments, missteps, and memories form a better picture than I could have ever calculated.

Picture this scene. You are at the beach on a beautiful, sunny day. There is a steady, cool breeze balanced by the sun's warmth. The sound of the waves and seagulls puts your heart in a calm, peaceful state. The scene is near perfect, but there is something happening down by the water.

There is a small child, maybe two years old. His father stands a short distance away. The child struggles to keep his plastic shovel from washing into the water. The father says, "Son, put the shovel farther up the beach away from the water." The son refuses, and the waves carry his little shovel back and forth on the sand.

The boy chases the shovel in frustration, looking as his father points farther up the beach away from the water, indicating his instruction is best.

Now, several people watch the scene unfold. There is another small child who thinks, "I'm gonna get that shovel if he loses it." A young boy, maybe nine or ten years old, thinks, "He should just keep holding the shovel, then the waves won't get it." A teenager sitting on a towel thinks, "Wow. That dad is such a jerk. Why doesn't he just help keep the shovel?" There is a young man sitting next to his new bride, and he thinks, "When I become a parent, my kid will do what I tell him." A man of about forty years of age watches with a grin. He thinks, "Wow. I remember when my kids were that age. It was so much easier then." Then, there is an elderly man next to his wife of fifty years. He thinks, "He is a good father. He is teaching his son to listen."

Different stages in life teach us to see things from a better vantage point. In the scenario above, we see how our perspective changes based on the seasons we have experienced. Sometimes, the greatest hindrance to our ability to see God's helping hand is our perception of what we think we want.

What if God's help is perfect and our expectation is not? Our ability to see God's help in our lives would change if we looked at our desires with healthy criticism. Just like a good parent doesn't give a child junk food at every request, God doesn't grant us every request. The old cliché is true: to learn to walk, we must fall down a few times. God's not really helping us learn to walk if he never lets us skin our knees.

The Apostle Paul taught this truth in the letter to Rome. In Romans 5:3-5 Paul writes, "Not only that, but we rejoice in our sufferings, knowing that suffering produces endurance, and endurance produces character, and character produces hope, and hope does not put us to shame, because God's love has been poured into our hearts through the Holy Spirit who has been given to us."

Let's go back to David from scripture. Before the story in the last chapter, God, through Samuel, anointed David to be the next king of Israel in 1 Samuel 16. David was told he would be the next king of Israel, and scripture says, "…And the Spirit of the LORD came powerfully upon David from that day on"(1 Samuel 16:13, NLT). Then, nothing happened. That's right. Samuel took off back to Ramah, and David went back to being a shepherd.

This has always struck me as a strange thing to happen. Being anointed king doesn't seem like going to a birthday party, and when the fun is over, everyone just goes back home. It seems like kind of a big deal.

The problem with David being anointed king and assuming the throne was that there was already a king sitting on it, Saul. He wasn't about to let this runt take his crown, as we saw in the last two chapters. Saul was going to fight for it. That would seem like a big problem for David. Only David didn't declare himself king. God did. So why didn't God just strike Saul dead with a bolt of lightning, or if that seemed a bit too flashy, no pun intended, why didn't he make Saul yield the throne at the very least. After all, God put Saul there; could he not also just remove him?

No. Instead, David spent years being tormented by a paranoid King Saul. He spent years living like a fugitive, worrying about his parents, who hid in the land of Moab for their own protection. David spent many nights sleeping on rocks, starving, and cold, yet go back to 1 Samuel 16:13 (NLT), "…And the Spirit of the LORD came powerfully upon David from that day on."

Was God helping David? At first glance, it is hard to give a clear affirmation. It looks like David was on his own despite having a God-given calling and the Spirit of the Lord in his life.

Have you ever felt that way? Have you ever felt like you were chasing the calling God has on your life, but every obstacle was in your way? Have you ever felt like you just wanted a little less bumpy road? Have you cried out for help from God and felt on your own? Have you ever cried out when your loved one suffered or when worry and fear clinched your heart so tightly life lost its beauty?

Despite the hardship, David seemed to feel a connection with God. Connecting with God is, I believe, one of the most significant pieces to seeing God's helping hand in our lives. When we connect with God through meditation, the Bible, and prayer, we begin understanding more about God's work in our lives, and we begin recognizing who God is and when he is working in us.

God is a teacher. Jesus, the incarnate of God Almighty, was even called "Rabbi." The best teachers introduce us to profound truths without us really knowing we are learning.

David had to learn to be the king God wanted him to be before he was to wear the crown. God helped him by teaching him the prerequisite for great things is the ability to bear great burdens. Great burdens weigh us down and create stress that almost inevitably produces some form of suffering.

While David was on the run from Saul, he experienced and endured many moments and types of suffering. There were certainly difficult days. Many days, David felt he was at the end of his rope, yet there is something worth noting about David's days on the run. Many Psalms seem to have been written during David's time fleeing. Many prayers were prayed. David had a closeness to God that dwarfed many other seasons in his life.

Think about this for a moment. David's greatest moral failure did not occur in his times of suffering. It was not from the mouth of a cave that David lusted after another man's wife. It was from the balcony of a palace, his palace. It was not until David seemingly had it all that his fleshly cravings for more were too much for him.

Like David, we long to leave the caves for the palace. We ask God to help us by moving us out of those seasons of being without. It is natural to want to leave the difficult and painful times in life, and I believe God wants to move us out of those times as well. But God doesn't want us to move out until we have gained a deep connection to him that will help us face the challenges in the higher places he has for us.

Much like David's time on the run from crazed King Saul, we are meant for more. Life is not about this temporary state of life here on Earth, but like all good training, it tests our limits for future application. For those in Jesus, there is an end to this temporary state. There is going to be a reuniting with all those we love and an end to death and pain. There is going to be a victory in your future, if you have chosen Jesus above this world.

Reflection:

1.　Are you currently in a season of suffering?
2.　Do you feel like you can connect with David's isolation and frustration?

3.	What lessons from David's exile as a fugitive helped him be a great king?

4.	What lessons do you think God can draw out of your current dark season for your future?

CHAPTER SIX
Looking for Help in All the Wrong Places

"Indeed, the LORD will give justice to his people,

and he will change his mind about his servants,

when he sees their strength is gone

and no one is left, slave or free.

Then he will ask, 'Where are their gods,

the rocks they fled to for refuge?

— Deuteronomy 32:36-37 (NLT)

Topic: We want to find help, but we often look in the wrong places.

When I was in college, a couple of buddies and I decided to go camping in the mountains on Halloween night. We lived about an hour from a state park in the Blue Ridge Mountains. So, we packed up my little Honda coupe and headed out late the day before Halloween.

As we started out of town, I wasn't too worried about getting fuel. I had around half of a tank, and my car was great on gas. Unfortunately for us, the conversation in the vehicle was far better than our sense of direction, and we took a wrong turn. We had no cell reception, and we had no idea where we were. We had driven significantly longer than our route was supposed to take, and we were between empty and a quarter of a tank of gas when we spotted a rickety sign for a gas station.

The decision to follow the sign got trickier, however, when we also saw a sign for the campground in the opposite direction. We decided to go to the gas station. We drove a few miles down a winding road while our imaginations pieced together cheesy horror movie situations we might find ourselves in just ahead.

Finally, we spotted the gas station. There were no lights. The closer we got, the less hope we had. The station was closed. It was early, too, maybe seven o'clock! Panic started to set in when I suggested we just shoot for the campground. We all agreed that if we ran out of gas at least we might have a chance to get help finding a ride at the campground.

We made it to the campground, but I'm sure my car was running on prayer and not gasoline. The next morning I coasted down the mountain toward the gas station that was closed the night before. When we got to the station, it was open! We gassed up and shared our story with the store owner. He laughed and said, "Yeah, when the sun goes down, we close up! You boys ain't used to that in the city now is ya?"

I was insulted because I'm not a city boy, but I did learn a valuable lesson. I will always gas up before I leave on a trip, and to this day, I do.

My friends and I found ourselves heading in the wrong direction, trying to find a solution, but in reality, we were just wasting more of the precious fuel we needed for the next day. Unfortunately, we often make the same mistakes with more important matters in life. We want to find help, but we often look in the wrong places, wasting our time and energy and making things harder when we should just turn to God.

In Exodus 32, the Bible tells us of the people of Israel making this mistake but in a magnified way. They not only looked for help in the wrong places, but they put their faith and worship in the wrong thing.

As a child, I never understood why the people of Israel would betray God by worshipping a golden calf that they made with their own hands. Surely, they would have known that anything they could make did not deserve to be worshipped. How could they pray to or believe in this handcrafted god?

Now, as an adult, I see the story differently. The people of Israel were not only stubborn, they were desperate. They no longer saw the structured system of Egypt around them. They saw nothing but wilderness. Their freedom came with responsibility, and their future now was uncertain.

The unknown, for most of us, is scary. These Israelites looked at their children and wondered what would happen to them. Even though they had witnessed the power and wonder of God in their lives, they gave their fear to uncertainty rather than deity. In Exodus 32:1, the path to idolatry for Israel came when they grew weary and fearful, during their waiting on the Lord. They told Aaron, "Up, make us gods who shall go before us. As for this Moses, the man who brought us up out of the land of Egypt, we do not know what has become of him." They would rather create a god than be patient with the real one.

The Israelites, in Exodus 32, modeled a pseudo-faith. While their lack of faith may seem ridiculous to us, we should not mock them. Instead, we should be convicted by their behavior because it is not very different from our own. The power behind making the statement, "I believe in the God of the Bible," has nearly vanished from most modern Christians, and we mimic this pseudo-faith of the Israelites. The reality of our "belief" is God may be real, but until He shows up, I'll do my own thing. I'll place my trust in something more visible, but I'll hope for something more spiritual.

Israel did not have trust in God while simultaneously worshipping a golden calf. They had a hope that there was power beyond themselves. If most people were honest, this is where many fall. They do not live as though a personal God exists, but they believe there is something beyond themselves. Many believe there is a higher power in the universe, but few truly accept that this power is a personal, relational God. As a result, when we say things like, "God help me," we aren't really talking to God, but we are expressing our desperation for help beyond our strength. This is problematic because to live in such a way is not the Bible's teaching, and I would argue that it is not our mind's natural way. We deeply need a personal relationship with our maker.

When we cry out to God for help, we are speaking to a being who has personal communication with us. This is not a generic higher power that may or may not care. This is a loving, personal God, the God of the Bible.

A cry from the depth of the human soul to his Almighty Maker should not be impersonal! It is deeply personal and emotional. The more personal a conversation, often the more beneficial and life changing it is.

Look at the account of David's repentance to God after he committed adultery and murder:

"Have mercy on me, O God,

according to your steadfast love;

according to your abundant mercy

blot out my transgressions.

Wash me thoroughly from my iniquity,

and cleanse me from my sin!

For I know my transgressions,

and my sin is ever before me.

Against you, you only, have I sinned

and done what is evil in your sight,

so that you may be justified in your words

and blameless in your judgment.

Behold, I was brought forth in iniquity,

and in sin did my mother conceive me.

Behold, you delight in truth in the inward being,

and you teach me wisdom in the secret heart."

— Psalm 51:1-6

David was raw and real before a holy God, and I believe this is, in part, why he had such a strong connection to God. David was in a mess, and he clearly wasn't living a perfect life. He poured out his heart on a personal level to a personal God. David didn't look to a ritualistic, phony exercise with a distant hope of finding forgiveness and healing. He looked to his deeply personal relationship with God. Consider these words for just a moment: "Behold, you delight in the truth in the inward being…" We MUST get back to this type of connection with God. David modeled for us that when we are in deep trouble, we aren't going to find our way out with shallow faith.

Many people feel helpless because they have been seeking help from false gods in the wrong places. Since everything about mankind is interpersonal, it is as ridiculous to believe in a "higher impersonal power" as it is to fashion an animal out of tin foil and worship it. The very preservation of our kind comes through interconnected, personal relations. The personal attributes of mankind are not required but are exhibited. I'm not required to have friends, but I do. I'm not required to be married, but I am. I'm not required to love my children, but I do. So why would I assume I'm made by a being who cares nothing about such things?

Like the Israelites, we create an image of God that we can fit into our understanding. We say things like, "How can God truly care about everyone?" To which I would say, the same way He created the atom. We ridiculously form an image that fits our minds, and then we are disappointed when things don't work out in the faith department.

Let me be as clear as possible. God does care and God wants to help you. Do you know this God, or have you been looking for help from a higher power? It is time to stop looking for help on your journey from a false, shallow faith in a false god. There is a real God, and he really wants to help you.

Reflection:

1. Consider the deepest relationships in your life. What qualities do they have?
2. Do you share those same qualities in your relationship with God?
3. What hurdles are stopping you from having a deep relationship with God?

CHAPTER SEVEN
Putting My Hands Where They Don't Belong

Humble yourselves before the Lord, and he will exalt you.

— James 4:10

Topic: God does not need our hand on his life; we need his hand on our lives.

I've never been a fan of inaction. So when a difficult situation arises, I want to help! I cannot stand back, feeling useless or helpless; however, God has taught me that there are times when he is working, and we need to keep our hands back. We must learn that on some occasions, the most helpful thing we can do is to minimize man's effort and watch God work. There are situations where we will only hurt ourselves and others by reaching into them.

In David's story in the Bible, there is an event that used to be difficult for me to stomach. In 2 Samuel 6, there is a man named Uzzah who was helping transport the Ark of the Covenant back to Jerusalem. Scripture says that the Ark was transported on a "new cart." Suddenly, the oxen stumbled. The Ark began to shift and Uzzah reached out to steady the Ark. "And the anger of the LORD was kindled against Uzzah, and God struck him down there because of his error, and he died there beside the ark of God" (2 Samuel 6:7).

David became angry with God over Uzzah's death, and if I'm honest, the first few times I read this, I was angry, too. Why, God? He was just trying to help. Are you not the God who is compassionate and slow to anger?

After praying over and studying the passage, this story became clearer. The Ark of the Covenant represented the very presence of God among sinners. Even though mankind had rebelled against God, God still wanted to connect with man. So he gave clear instructions through the Levitical systems of how people could still connect with him, though they had sinned against him.

When Jesus came, he was perfect but took upon himself the sin of us all. The Ark did not bear sin. It remained untouched by sin as a holy instrument of God's presence among man. As Numbers 4:15 tells us, it could not be touched. When Uzzah reached out to stable the Ark, he reached into a situation that his hand was not capable of helping. God does not need our hand on his life; we need his hand on our lives.

When we put our hands on God's perfect plan, we mess it up! It seems, without a doubt, that Uzzah had only good intentions. He wanted to stop the Ark from falling. He obviously cared about the things of God because of his willingness to help; however, God wants us to trust His hand and His plan.

If Uzzah and David had spent more time seeking God's way of transporting the Ark, this tragedy would have never happened. Often, if we would spend more time seeking God's way in our own lives, we could avoid some of the pain we experience as well.

The Ark of the Covenant of God was never supposed to be on that "new cart." It was supposed to be carried by Levites holding the wooden poles that were on both sides of the Ark (See Exodus 25:10-16). For whatever reason, David put the Ark on a cart, like the Philistines.

David, in his hiding from Saul, had spent some time living in Ziklag in the Philistine territory. In fact, he even marched with the Philistine armies until he was asked to leave by the king because he wasn't trusted by some of the Philistine leaders. David had spent time with the enemies of Israel, and maybe that influenced him more than we would like to admit.

If you spend enough time listening to the culture you're in, you will allow it to dictate more of your life than maybe it should. There is nothing wrong with being in a culture. There is nothing wrong with admiring a culture, but there is something wrong with letting the culture determine your morals. If you are a Christian, the moral standard is found within the Bible. It's God's standard that holds weight eternally.

Maybe David used the cart because he wanted to expedite the process. Maybe David felt that the cart was more efficient, easier, and logical. Well, I guess we can't argue there, but where did God ever tell us that His plan was efficient, easy, and logical? In fact, there are consistent messages in scripture that communicate that God's plan completely flies in the face of efficiency, ease, and logic.

God does not need to fit within our budget of time, difficulty, and logic. He isn't interested in that at all. God makes clear that he loves us, and he cares more deeply for us than simply giving us an efficient, easy, and logical life. He wants us to develop and grow. That often comes through things that are difficult and hard to understand.

It is interesting that Uzzah's name means "strength." If doing God's will was wholly dependent on man's strength, it would make perfect sense for every situation to be weighed by efficiency, difficulty, and logic. Those are reasonable considerations for our abilities, but God's plan doesn't depend on man's strength. It is, in fact, beyond man's capability. When we try to interject our hands with our limitation of strength onto God's plan, we are certain to see a sad result.

In David's case, he got laser-focused on getting the Ark to Jerusalem, and He neglected to consult with God about how to do it. I cannot help but believe this is often true in many churches today. We want to help, and we begin lots of programs, events, and plans. We start developing strategies to grow our churches and restore spiritual health in our congregations, but we neglect God's instruction. Just like God had instructions for carrying the Ark, he has instructions for doing church.

God doesn't need our growth development strategy or our five-step process. God doesn't need us to hire the church growth expert. We need to stop reaching into God's territory with our hands. Instead, we need God to reach his hand in to touch our hearts. We can have healthy, growing churches by getting back to the model in scripture.

Church can be simple. We can focus back on God and not on who leads the committee or which deacon hurts our feelings. We can start loving each other as Jesus instructed instead of backbiting and cold-shouldering. Like David, many churches and church leaders have experienced tragedy because we have neglected to simply surrender to God's way instead of our own way.

The temptation to use our own strength in God's plan goes beyond church as well with another institution of God: the family. We cannot hold our families together with big houses, big incomes, and luxury cars. God is essential to a healthy family unit. If we subtract him from the equation, we are destined to receive a disappointing result. We mistakenly believe that if we can get our kids into a certain school, enroll them into a particular program, or they could become star athletes, we are on the road to being successful parents. Unfortunately, the human soul cannot be purified by human hands. We need a holy God. We need that holy God in our homes, and we need him in our families. Ultimately, each individual has to choose to follow him, including our children, but it is by him and through him that a healthy family and home life exists.

Are you trying to use your strength to hold your life together? Are you weary from the constant weight you are trying to hold? Maybe God is helping you see your need for his strength. Maybe you have wrestled to the point of exhaustion so you can have him show you where your abilities meet their boundaries. Let God's hand handle the things beyond your strength. Welcome his help and trust. He will provide it.

Reflection:

1. Reflect for a moment about your life. Are there areas of your life where you are not trusting God's helping hand?
2. Are there areas in your life where you are putting your strength in God's process?
3. Are you assuming God's way is efficient, easy, and logical?

CHAPTER EIGHT
The Surrender Prayer

And he withdrew from them about a stone's throw, and knelt down and prayed, saying, "Father, if you are willing, remove this cup from me. Nevertheless, not my will, but yours, be done."

— Luke 22:41-42

Topic: We need to surrender our lives to God. And God can use even our mistakes to help each other in life.

There is a big difference between a Christian and a surrendered Christian. I learned this lesson very early in life because I became a Christian at age twelve, but I did not surrender to Jesus until I was in college. When I first became a Christian, I recognized what Jesus did for me on the cross, but I didn't surrender to the idea of what I could do for him.

Many believers get stuck in the infant Christian stage. The Apostle Paul even addressed this in his letter to the Corinthian church (1 Corinthians 3:1-8). Many believers don't realize that Christianity is far deeper than simply eternal security. It is beginning a relationship with the God who authored the universe. How incredible is that! The God who is bigger than the universe cares for you and desires a personal relationship with you. He wants to teach you things. He wants to watch you grow as a person, and he wants you involved in his work. It is truly amazing.

As we grow in our faith, we realize Christianity is not only about what God did for us, but it is also about what he wants to do through us. He has included us in his purposes. He has a larger plan at work than we could possibly comprehend, but he will not force us to be involved. You can refuse to surrender to God's purpose for you as his child, but I warn you that you will wish that you had just done things God's way. This, I believe, is the difference between a surrendered Christian and a wayward one.

We can also see this misstep in David's life. David was a man after God's own heart. He faced giants with a bold faith, and his closeness to God saturates the Psalms. Still, he didn't surrender to God's way in one season of his life, and it led to one tragedy after the other. In 2 Samuel 11:1, we read, "In the spring of the year, the time when kings go out to battle, David sent Joab, and his servants with him, and all Israel. And they ravaged the Ammonites and besieged Rabbah. But David remained at Jerusalem." David was the king, but he didn't fulfill his duty this year. David's lack of surrender to the position God called him to serve led to an affair, murder, incest, rape, and years of family division.

Mistakenly, many believe that choosing to trust in Jesus and the gospel removes the temptation to walk in our own way. However, surrendering to God's calling upon our lives is ongoing. Jesus told us the parable of the prodigal son, and I believe the parable has multiple applications. However, one thing I see in that parable is the story of surrender and returning to the father. I believe that it is entirely possible to live with the Holy Spirit in your heart but walk in the wrong direction.

I write about this from a place of experience, unfortunately. In this chapter, I will write about some of the most painful times in my life. I've never shared some of the things you will read in this chapter from the pulpit (at least not at the time I'm writing this) because these wounds have not fully healed. My sole purpose in this chapter is that I know God can use even our mistakes to help each other in life. I pray my mistakes will help you.

Much like the prophet Jonah, I often run from God's calling and plan. Why? I'm not sure. Sometimes, I believe it is pride, believing I have a better route than even God (yes, I'm that stupid). Sometimes, I'm simply afraid. Sometimes, I'm just rebellious. No matter the reason, I'm an expert at running from God's plan. I spent several years without surrender, and I'm here to warn you against my behavior.

When I first felt a calling to ministry, I quickly dismissed it. I'm introverted, and most pastors I know are anything but introverted. I also knew nothing about being a pastor. I don't come from a long line of ministers. The first time that I ever shared a Bible story in front of a group of people was in my high school homeroom.

I attended a Christian high school, and the opportunity came, my senior year, for me to share a devotional in front of my peers. So, I shared from John 13. It is the passage that records Jesus washing the disciples' feet. Something happened inside of me, and I became overwhelmed with emotion. I began fighting back tears as I shared the words of the scripture that recorded Jesus washing the filthy feet of the disciples. My Lord and my Savior bowed low at the feet of sinners. I shared how much that meant to me with my class, and to this day, I hope it helped my dear classmates at Carolina Christian Academy.

Later that day, a teacher came and asked if I had ever thought about becoming a pastor. I became somewhat angry on the inside at his question. I thought, "Who does he think he is to plant that thought in my head! I'm no pastor!"

My senior year I ended up preaching a sermon at a fine arts festival. I told the judges in the back of the room at the beginning of my message, "I'm not here to get some sort of score or grade. I'm here to share what

God has on my heart." I meant it, and I pray I never preach for the pleasure or satisfaction of people.

Despite the signs and feelings in my life, I quickly dismissed anyone who suggested I go to school to study to become a minister. I wanted nothing to do with it. I really couldn't describe the complexities of why I felt that way, but I now know that the best thing I can say about my attitude is it was utter rebellion. God was doing something inside me, and I had not surrendered to that work.

As I began college, I did so as a biology major. I was a horrible biology major, but out of that season, I met my wonderful wife. She was studying to become a pharmacist, and I was trying to survive chemistry. Through a series of trials, which I touched upon in the introduction, I found myself at a low point in my life. I believe it was the first time that I began my battle with depression, but more on that later.

One evening, I came back to my dorm room, and I began to weep. I felt completely broken, as though I was staring life in the face, and I had nothing to offer it. I had no feeling about why God made me. I thought about the future, and I felt there was no hope for an average Joe like me. At that moment, I felt a sweet peace and presence. I felt the presence of God, and I knew He was with me.

Then I prayed from a place of brokenness, "God, I will do your will. I will do things your way, but please help me." The following week, I changed my major from biology to Christian theology. In my mind, I was "burning the ships," as Hernan Cortes was rumored to have done in 1519 as he stepped on the sands of Central America. There would be no turning back, but as I walked down the stairs of the Merritt Administration building at Anderson University, I felt overwhelmed with fear. My eyes watered as I held my change of major form in hand. Then I whispered under my breath, "God help me do this. Please, God. I need your help now. I don't know what I'm doing."

In my mind, I had just given up on my plan. I really had no clue what you do with a Christian theology degree. I felt scared and uncertain. Thoughts quickly rushed into my mind, "What if you just messed up your future? This could be the mistake of your life."

Within a few hours, I received a phone call from a church near my hometown. It was the pastor of the church, and he shared his name, then told me something I will never forget. He told me that he had an anonymous recommendation two weeks prior that I should be considered as their summer student worker. That marked the beginning of my ministry.

Having grown up in church, I had been told that God would help me, but it wasn't until I had the experience of God's assistance in my life that I truly believed that God was helping me. When I surrender to God's plan, he will help me carry it out. I mark that as a time when I learned the value of having a surrender prayer.

If you are struggling and crying out to God for help, have you had a surrender prayer? I'm not talking about accepting the truth of the gospel. I'm talking about a moment in your Christian life when you have talked to God about his plan taking priority over yours.

Jesus modeled a prayer exactly like this in Luke 22:39-42. Jesus shared with God the Father a deep and intimate prayer moment in this passage. He said, "Father, if you are willing, remove this cup from me. Nevertheless, not my will, but yours, be done." In other words, Jesus told God that the priority was not his will but it was his Father's will. Have you done that in your life?

I encourage you to take a moment and have that time with God, especially if you find yourself in a current struggle or battle. There is something incredible that takes place when we lay our will at His feet. Let me give one caveat: it must not merely be words, but it must come from an authentic desire for God's plan to be the top agenda of your existence.

Now, let me also share that I have learned that the surrender prayer doesn't end the fight. If anything, it begins a battle. When you lay down your will, your sinful nature wants to pick it right back up. I wish I could tell you that was the end of the chapter, and after you surrender to God's will, life gets easy. Unfortunately, that has not been my reality, and I dare say it won't be your story either.

Since I began in ministry, I have constantly wrestled with my will. This is the part of the story I have never really spoken out loud to anyone except my wife (again, at least this is true at the time of my writing). The darkest days of my ministry have come when I stepped into my will while trying to hold onto God's plan. I've learned this valuable lesson, and I pray, friend, that you heed this warning: You cannot do God's plan your way.

After several years of youth ministry, I was called to serve in a lead pastor role at a small, rural church. I was there for several years. It was filled with kind, loving people. I was truly blessed by them, and I will always be grateful for the first church I pastored: Beaver Creek Baptist Church. I had great friendships, and the church was doing well. One November day, I walked inside the parsonage, and I looked at my wife and said, "It is time for me to resign."

I felt God leading me to make a move, but instead of praying, seeking, and patiently listening, I started planning my next move. I had always wanted to serve in the military, and I have always admired the soldiers who sacrificed so much for us to enjoy the freedoms we have. So, I began pursuing military chaplaincy, and I resigned from my role as pastor.

Through many setbacks, I eventually made it into the U.S. Army Chaplain Corps. I first became a U.S. Army Reserve chaplain, but this, I am now certain, was not God's plan for me. Instead, this was my will and desire. The same sweet, peaceful presence that led me to ministry seemed distant in my pursuit of this role.

Years passed in my process to enter the military chaplaincy, and during this time I had become miserable not serving in a pastoral role. After a couple of years, I felt compelled to return to the pulpit, and I would have to try to make both the chaplaincy and the pastorate work together. I began pastoring another small, rural church just before I was accepted into the Army chaplaincy and given my duty assignment. I immediately felt torn between my ministry there and my ministry as a chaplain. I began to feel like I did in my dorm room that night of my first surrender prayer in my Christian journey. I felt like I was letting so many people down, and I never felt like I was giving the chaplaincy or my church all of me.

Through many internal battles of the mind, I found myself feeling depressed nearly every day. One day, I got up and began my routine with my happy face, but on the inside, I had allowed my thoughts to wander way too far off course. I began imagining the world without me in it and if it would be better for everyone. I had allowed our enemy, the devil, to deceive me into thinking that my path was best, and now he was mocking me for finding myself lost with no direction. He was telling me that I was nothing. He was convincing me that I could not help anyone in any way.

Hopelessness had begun to grip me day after day, and I had just about reached the point of believing the devil's lies. That is a dangerous place, friend. I had seriously begun contemplating suicide, and I had never believed that would have been my fate. I reached out to an Army resource, who helped me tremendously. I did, however, spend a week away from my family in a mental health facility.

Broken, confused, and alone, I sat and stared at an empty, white wall. I believed that all of my ministry was over. After all, who wants a pastor or chaplain with suicidal thoughts? I requested a Bible from a nurse in that facility, and she got me a copy of Gideon's Bible. I cherished it. For hours on end, I sat and read that Bible. God spoke to my heart just like he did that night in my dorm.

Once again, I had my surrender prayer. I said, "Father, I am broken because I have done things my way again. Lord, I have nothing to lay before you except what's left of me. But here I am. If you still can use me, I'll do your will, not mine. God help me." Once again, a feeling of peace filled my heart, and a presence filled my room. God helped me. He brought me out of that dark thinking. He not only restored my mind, but He also restored my ministry!

I stepped down from my role as a military chaplain, and I returned to a full focus on civilian pastoral work. But I learned something of great value. Even in my mistakes and pain, God loved me, and He will use our mistakes for the greater good. My training in the Army has served as a tremendous help to me, and I gained much-needed confidence from serving alongside my brothers and sisters in the military.

If you find yourself feeling like you wandered from God's path for you, there is hope. I do not know God's journey for you, and I do not know the pain you've experienced. There is one thing of which I'm certain. God loves us. Even when we walk away from His will to accommodate our own plan, He loves us.

God loves us in a truly incomprehensible way. I think most of us in Christian communities have lost a deep sense of awe at that incredible truth, and many have not truly embraced the wonders of such a thing. God loves us.

The God who authored the cosmos loves you and me. He cares for us deeply. No. I mean it! Don't just read that line without giving pause to the grandeur of it. He loves you so much that he has specific purposes for just you in a world of billions of souls, making each one significant. He loves you so much that he knows the number of hairs on your head. He loves you so much that he has given you gifts and talents. Most importantly, he loves you so much that he sent his one and only Son, Jesus, to die for you. God loves us.

Perhaps you are in a very dark place right now, and you are crying out to him. God will help you, but you cannot expect God to help you walk down a road that is not best for you or those around you. He will help you turn around and experience a different way, but have you surrendered to him? Have you let go of your way? Before going to the next chapter, I pray you will have that surrender prayer.

Reflection:

1. Do you feel that you are broken beyond repair? There is no such thing as our God!
2. Take a moment to consider how God has pieced your life together. Think of broken relationships, past pains, or failures.
3. God is not wasteful. He will use it all if you hand it over to him. Will you?
4. Take a moment to surrender the burdens of your heart. He will pick up the pieces.

CHAPTER NINE
Help Intercepted

"Let all bitterness and wrath and anger and clamor and slander be put away from you, along with all malice. Be kind to one another, tenderhearted, forgiving one another, as God in Christ forgave you."

— Ephesian 4:31–32

Topic: Anger and bitterness hurt your relationship with God and prevent his help.

In the past few years, I have really gotten into working in the yard. I built a retaining wall, put in a couple of mulch beds, and planted some flowers. I put edging around a flower bed in my yard last year. As my grass grew, I noticed it slowly creeping under my edging, invading my flower bed despite having put up a barrier to keep it out.

Sometimes, anger and bitterness work this way. They slowly creep into our lives despite putting up barriers to keep them out. Anger is tricky. I certainly believe there are times when anger is appropriate. The problem is that anger is hard to tame. If anger is not kept on a short, disciplined leash, it quickly gets out of control. Many times it converts into a grudge, laced in bitterness. The Bible tells us that we must put those things out of our life (Ephesians 4:31). We cannot allow even the smallest amount of bitterness because it will spread and take over our hearts.

In David's story, we've discussed King Saul's hatred for David, but where did it begin? In 1 Samuel 18:6-9, we read the origin of Saul's hatred. As King Saul and David returned from their victory over the Philistine army, the Israelite people welcomed them with singing and dancing. Their song was: "Saul has struck down his thousands, and David his ten thousands."

The seed of jealousy was planted in Saul's heart that day. It grew into bitterness. Saul's bitterness for David became a wall between him and God. Saul quickly stopped searching for what God wanted for Israel, and he turned to his own agenda. Eliminating David became more important than elevating God's name above every name.

When bitterness begins invading our hearts, we not only have a sour relationship with someone, but we interrupt the work God is doing in our lives. Despite all of my work to plant my rose bushes, spread mulch, and build a retaining wall, the focal point on my flower bed was the invading grass. Even though you may feel you are making progress in your spiritual walk, the focal point when bitterness invades is the frustration, anger, or even hate you have for someone in your life.

If you are crying out to God for help and feel you are getting nowhere, ask yourself if you have bitterness in your life. It may be possible that the person God has sent into your life to help you is the very person you have bitterness toward. It may also be possible that the bitterness in your life has become a wedge between you and God. It is fully possible that you are deeply angry and cannot see the help God is sending your way because you are focused on anger. I do not know your situation, but I can guarantee this: if there is bitterness in you, then you are limiting your ability to receive God's helping hand.

I have found that the very act of forgiveness is helpful to the soul. There is a burden lifted when we let go of bitterness and anger. It frees us and helps us deal with challenges without having our focus divided.

Some years ago, I had an individual in my life who was difficult for me. Maybe he felt the same way about me, but I kept finding this person in the middle of controversy with those around him. He had an abrasive and dominant personality, and he always seemed to want to spend time with me. Every time I was around him, I felt like I was walking on eggshells, and I was uncomfortable when he would mention people we both knew.

The relationship I had with this person became frustrating for me because of the constant controversy that surrounded him. Rarely did our conversations begin on a positive note. On several occasions, he said things to me that I felt were deliberate, hurtful attacks. I started watering seeds of bitterness in my heart by storing offenses in my head of the times I felt wronged by him. Then, my heart took a turn in the wrong direction.

One night, my wife worked a late shift over an hour from our home, and she did not get home until well into the morning hours. I stayed awake because I did not want to go to sleep while she was on the road.

The next morning, this same person was banging on my door at six o'clock. When I answered the door, I clearly looked as though I had jumped from my bed (because I did). I was greeted by this fellow who said, "Good morning. I thought you said you like to get up early, but it doesn't look like it. Hurry up and get ready. I wanna talk to ya about some work we are thinking about doing."

I bit my tongue, got dressed, and didn't complain. The worst part was that my heart was fuming, but my face wore a mask. I did not share my frustration, but I dumped fertilizer onto the bitterness growing in me toward this person. He eventually became a person that I gossiped to my wife about when I was angry, and I could only see the bad things he did instead of the good. Instead of confronting him about the offenses that bothered me and openly sharing my frustration, I acted hypocritically. I viewed him as an enemy, but I treated him like an ally. My dishonesty and deception only encouraged bitterness in my heart toward the man.

Eventually, he left the church I pastored, and we moved away as well. I found myself often bringing up his name in a negative way. I sometimes would think of him and get angry. I would often wish that I could run into him and "give him a piece of my mind." Eventually, God convicted my heart quite strongly about it. I knew I had a bitterness problem.

One evening, the man called me and left a voicemail on my phone. We had not spoken in years, but he was working on a project and had a specific question for me. At first, I was reluctant to call him back, but God clearly prompted my heart to do so. I needed to make things right with this man, and the grudge needed to be let go. So I called him back.

We had a great phone conversation. I told him I was sorry for not being a better friend, and in his own way, he apologized to me. I gave forgiveness, but I gained freedom. I stopped carrying around the painful past, and I now could see how God used this man to help my ministry. This man helped me in so many ways, and all the while, I could not see that God was preparing me for things ahead.

Bitterness had blinded me to the work God was doing in me. Bitterness has a way of keeping us from seeing the bigger picture and being open to God's help. The Apostle Paul wrote in Ephesians that we should put away these things from ourselves and we must adopt a new approach. Instead of bitterness, we are to "be kind to one another, tenderhearted, forgiving one another as God in Christ forgave you" (Ephesians 4:32 [ESV]).

Saul's bitterness toward David simmered until his own death. Saul's story is a tragic one because he was a man, anointed by God, but controlled by his pride. Instead of Saul becoming a good king, he became a bitter leader. He sought his own agenda. Instead of Saul seeing God's best for his people, Saul could only see through the lens of hate, and his life and family line tragically ended.

Maybe bitterness has crept into your life. Maybe it has been limiting your ability to see what God is doing. Maybe God is helping you through the difficult people in your life, but the bitterness you have toward them is stopping you from seeing how. I encourage you to think about those you may have bitterness toward and remember that Jesus forgave you. We must forgive them. You will find freedom in forgiveness, and you may find that the helping hand of God often works through the things and people that irritate us.

Reflection:

1. Is there someone who came to your mind in this chapter? Do you have a bitterness developing against them?
2. How might God be using this person to help you?
3. What are you holding onto that you need to let go?
4. What would your life look like if you stopped feeling frustrated through bitterness toward people?

CHAPTER TEN

If You Knew Then What You Know Now

For freedom Christ has set us free; stand firm therefore, and do not submit again to a yoke of slavery.

— Galatians 5:1

Topic: One of the most significant ways God helps us is by giving us a clearer picture of the truly valuable things.

There are so many times in life that we look back and wish we had chosen to do things differently. Right now, there are dozens of situations, events, and investments that immediately pop into my mind. I often find myself looking back on things, playing Monday morning quarterback with life decisions.

My grandfather says often, "We always have 20-20 vision when we look back." Isn't it funny how experience and life's lessons help us gain a better perspective? Not only do we see things more clearly, looking back, but we also value things more appropriately.

I spent a short time as a hospice chaplain, and I got to know many people at the end of their lives. I was so blessed to spend time with some of those wonderful people before they departed this world. I can also tell you that being given a terminal diagnosis will bring clarity to the things that are valuable in life. I never heard a single hospice patient share with me that they wish they had worked more overtime, but I heard many say they wished they had spent more time with those they loved.

One of the most significant ways God helps us is by giving us a clearer picture of the truly valuable things. When we learn to identify the truly valuable, we start prioritizing the right way. The result is that we feel we are investing ourselves appropriately in life. The writer of Ecclesiastes gives the reader a sobering reality about life in Ecclesiastes 2:9-11:

So I became great and surpassed all who were before me in Jerusalem. Also, my wisdom remained with me. And whatever my eyes desired I did not keep from them. I kept my heart from no pleasure, for my heart found pleasure in all my toil, and this was my reward for all my toil. Then I considered all that my hands had done and the toil I had expended in doing it, and behold, all was vanity and a striving after wind, and there was nothing to be gained under the sun.

The writer of Ecclesiastes had gone where many long to go. He had everything the world had to offer, yet he was still empty. His conclusion on this life was that all is vanity. The only real joy, purpose, and hope we have is in God Almighty. This provokes the question: Are you pursuing a goal that you will look back and be proud to have chased? Will that goal matter in eternity?

God can help you build a life on things that matter, but we must first realize there are some things that don't. We must learn to see things that have value, but that can be harder than it sounds. Perhaps no one knows this lesson better than a man named John Reed.

Many years ago, there was a German immigrant named John Reed. Reed settled down in North Carolina, in what we know now as Cabarrus County. It was there that he and his family worked hard to manage a small farm.

Making a living on a small farm, in those times especially, wasn't easy, but Reed squeaked by to provide for his family. One Sunday morning, John and his wife went to church, but they had to leave their children under the care of their eldest son, Conrad, because they only had one horse.[4]

While Conrad Reed and his two younger siblings played in Little Meadow Creek, they noticed a large, bright-colored rock that was really heavy. The kids

---

[4] Carolina Gold Rush, Bruce Roberts. McNally and Loftin Publishers, Charlotte, NC. 1971, pg 5.

brought the 17-pound stone home to their father. John asked a local silversmith about the stone, but he was informed that it had no real value. For three years, the stone was used as a doorstop. The true value of the stone was eventually realized, and it would go into the record books as one of the largest gold nuggets found in the United States.[5]

Sometimes, the true value of something cannot be known until it is seen with the right set of eyes. John Reed saw a doorstop, but what he truly had was a treasure. Maybe you have miscalculated the value of things in your life. Maybe you are missing out on some really valuable blessings God has right in front of you while you pursue something far less important. John Reed walked right past a fortune every day for three years to make a small profit on his mediocre farm. What are you missing in your life that is a blessing you don't recognize?

For me, I'm learning to enjoy moments with my children. I have been told that I shouldn't blink because they'll be grown. Therefore, I'm trying to cherish time with them. I don't want to wake up one day and realize that I didn't recognize being a dad is a huge blessing.

I'm also recognizing that you must cherish friendships. The great friends in our lives understand

---

[5] Ibid., 5.

when we must prioritize certain responsibilities ahead of them; however, if we are not careful, we are not there for them when they really need us. I'm learning to value my great friends, and if that means pressing pause or missing something to support a friend in need, I'm going to try to do it.

Let us help ourselves to not look back on our lives with regret. Maybe we need to carve time out of our day and pray that God would give us eyes to spot the value in what he is doing in our lives. Sometimes, the greatest help we can receive is a different perspective.

Reflection:

1. If you were to make a list of the top five blessings in your life, what would they be?
2. If you look over that list, are you valuing these things like they are the top five blessings?
3. What are some ways you can organize time for the valuable things in your life?

CHAPTER ELEVEN
Right on Time

So the LORD must wait for you to come to him

so he can show you his love and compassion.

For the LORD is a faithful God.

Blessed are those who wait for his help.

— Isaiah 30:18 (NLT)

Topic: God's timing is perfect.

There is a principle that I'm learning about God's helping hand. It doesn't come early, and it doesn't come late. Like Gandalf in Lord of the Rings, "He arrives precisely when he means to!"

One of the lessons David shared in the Psalms is to trust God's timing. In Psalm 27:14, David shared, "Wait for the LORD; be strong, and let your heart take courage; wait for the LORD!" In this short little verse, we have a great command: "Wait for the Lord!" Why did David tell us to wait? It is because David knew God's timing is perfect.

Sometimes, it is extremely difficult to embrace God's timing. It is especially difficult when you are crying out for help, and it feels like God is running late.

I'm the type of person who enjoys arriving early. I like to arrive fifteen minutes prior to everything, and if I'm not there by then, my anxiety roars. Scripture teaches us that God doesn't operate on our timetable. Rather, God has a perfect schedule.

For a flawed person who fears being late, I sometimes feel like God is supposed to be like me. Sometimes, I feel like God doesn't show up early enough, but God knows something I do not. God has a better vantage point, and God isn't looking at my life inside of time. God's helping hand extends precisely when it should because he knows the exact moment his hand is most needed.

God's helping hand is punctual, arriving at the precise point. There is an amazing story in the gospels that is a great reminder of this truth. In Matthew 14:22-33, the gospel writer tells us the disciples of Jesus were on the sea when a fierce wind began to blow, with sea mist clouding their eyes. Up and down the large waves, the disciples gripped the boat. Suddenly, one of the disciples spotted something that sent a chill up his spine. There, in the darkness, was a figure walking upon the water. He couldn't find the words for a moment as his mouth dropped open. Then he shouted, "It's a ghost!" Another disciple spotted the same unexplained sight and joined in with affirmation, "It is! Look! There is a ghost!"

Then, across the angry waves, a familiar voice spoke, "Don't be afraid. Take courage. I am here." It was the voice of Jesus. Finding an indescribable strength and faith from the moment, Peter shouted to Jesus, "Lord, if it's really you, tell me to come to you, walking on the water." Jesus replied, "Yes, come."

Peter did the unthinkable. He left the boat, stepping onto the dark water and angry waves. His feet did not penetrate the water, and he did what only Jesus had done. He began walking on the water. The moment was nothing shy of amazing. Peter experienced something that no one else has experienced since that day. The bold faith that got Peter out of the boat brought him to a place of astonishment and wonder, but it also brought him to a place of uncertainty.

The Bible tells us that Peter "...Saw the strong wind and waves, he was terrified and began to sink." He then cried out one of the shortest prayers in all of scripture, but it was perhaps also one of the most profound, "Save me, Lord." Matthew 14:31 (NLT) then records what happened, "Jesus immediately reached out and grabbed him. 'You have so little faith,' Jesus said. 'Why did you doubt me?' "

Jesus did not act the moment Peter made a mistake, nor did he when fear took over. He reacted the moment Peter asked him to save him. That moment was perfect. It was then Peter saw the power of prayer.

It was then Peter appreciated the saving power of the hand of God. He realized the wind and waves were no match for their maker. It was not a moment too soon or too late.

If we really want to get to the heart of the story, we must look at a keyword Jesus used to describe Peter's struggle on the sea. The key word is *doubt*. The Greek word used by the author of the gospel was *distazo*. It is formed from the root *duo*, meaning "two." In a literal sense, the word means caught between two points. Peter was literally caught between two points or masters: the boat and Jesus.

Peter had been a fisherman, and for years, he had been on the sea. He had seen his share of storms, but never had he walked on the sea. The uncertainty of leaving the familiar, the boat, to walk on the waves was an act of faith.

Peter began in a good direction with a good intention, but in his attempt to draw close to Jesus, despite the impossible odds in his way, he lost sight of his goal. He became concerned with where he was, and he was concerned with what was against him. So, he doubted. He froze between where Jesus told him to be and the familiar boat.

You may wonder what this has to do with God's timing, and the answer is everything (Yoda accent applied)! God let Peter discover what it is like to take a step of faith, to walk by faith, and to sink in doubt.

Jesus was teaching Peter that he would be there when Peter's faith was small and his prayer desperate. Jesus was teaching Peter that he would reach into the overwhelming circumstances of his life. Also, Jesus was teaching Peter that he had the power to save him when he could not save himself and the importance of focusing on him.

Sometimes, the most important part of God's timing is that he shows us what we cannot do. Recently, I had some time to do a unique devotion. I sat on my couch with a legal pad, and I wrote down a list of things that I couldn't do. I know. It seems a little like a downer, but I promise it has merit. My goal was to put on paper my limits.

There is this idea that you should never fail or admit it when you do. That is ludicrous. We need to find our limits. We need to discover the edge of our strength. I remember working out with a friend in college who did not count his repetitions. He simply went until he failed. He found that he'd give up based on a number rather than his ability. So he just did his exercises until he could do no more. I hated working out with him, but I think he had a way of pushing himself that taught me something. We have to discover where we find our limits.

My devotional exercise taught me that by writing down what I could not do I knew the source of my stress and struggle. I was trying to accomplish things beyond my strength. I need help. I need divine help that does not grow faint or weary (Isaiah 40:28).

Jesus let Peter sink, but he didn't let Peter drown. His timing let Peter feel the wind and waves, but he also let Peter feel his strength pulling him up. His timing showed Peter what he couldn't do, but it revealed to Peter what God's strength could do. One moment, he was drowning with no hope, and in the next moment, he was locked, hand-in-hand, with the maker of the universe, and nothing could touch him.

All of these lessons came because Jesus didn't show up early. He waited for the strong wind. He didn't show up too late and miss the disciples in the middle of the heavy waves. No. Jesus showed up in the middle of their struggle and called out to them. He showed them a miracle, and he taught profound lessons. His timing was perfect.

Are you struggling with God's timing? Are you crying out for help, but you feel like God isn't showing up? Take a deep breath, and speak this truth: God's timing is perfect. The Holy Spirit of God is with every believer. Through His Holy Spirit, God is doing things in your life with precision. It may not appear so from an earthly lens, but remember you are eternal. Your soul will go on for eternity, and God is giving you essential lessons that will play a part in who you are even beyond your life on this Earth.

Reflection:

1. Take a moment with God, and write down things you cannot do. By discovering the end of your strength, you find a way to inevitably wait for the Lord. Take this time to pray over the areas of your life where you have to trust God's timing.
2. Has God ever been late?
3. Embrace the truth of his perfection and your limitations, recognizing his timing is perfect.

CHAPTER TWELVE

God Help Me Love People

But I say, walk by the Spirit, and you will not gratify the desires of the flesh

— Galatians 5:16

Topic: God helps you love because you CANNOT fully love people through your perspective.

Before I go anywhere in this chapter, I need to share the truth about loving others. Here is the truth: you CANNOT fully love people through your perspective. I know this statement is not fun to read, and the knee-jerk reaction is to say, "Yes, I can!" Give me a few paragraphs to explain, and then you can disagree if you'd like.

First, let's go to the Bible. In 1 Corinthians 13:4-7, the Bible defines love:

"[4] Love is patient and kind; love does not envy or boast; it is not arrogant [5] or rude. It does not insist on its own way; it is not irritable or resentful; [6] it does not rejoice at wrongdoing, but rejoices with the truth. [7] Love bears all things, believes all things, hopes all things, endures all things."

Think for a moment about what it means to be selfish. Selfishness is "starting and ending with one's self". Love is "placing self aside". What does it mean to be patient? It means to delay self-gratification. What does it mean to be kind? It means to give someone something that is not benefiting self in the action. What does it mean to be arrogant? It means thinking highly of one's self. What does it mean to be rude? It means appeasing one's own desires or thoughts without regard for another. Then, we have the direct address to self in the next line of the passage, "It does not insist on its own way."

We could keep going, but I think you get the picture. Love requires us to look beyond ourselves, and therefore, if we look at others through our own lens, we don't really get love. Galatians 5:17 tells us, "For the desires of the flesh are against the Spirit, and the desires of the Spirit are against the flesh, for these are opposed to each other, to keep you from doing the things you want to do." Our flesh tends to get in the way of truly loving others. The flesh wants to satisfy self, and the Spirit of God living within us tells us that self is not paramount. Therefore, we must be careful not to confuse love with self-satisfaction.

The picture Paul painted for us as he wrote this letter to the Church at Corinth is that love is outside of self-gratification, a greater concept. The original Greek word used in this text is *agape*, which can be chosen at the expense of one's self. It is the word we would use to describe God's love. The deepest form of love is revealed by a perfect creator sending his one and only son to die for his rebellious creation.

Just the other night, on the couch, my wife and I were talking, and I was complaining about the limitations of the English language compared to some of the ancient writings. I shared with her that we just don't have enough specification with some words in English compared to Greek. It would have been a perfect moment for me to be romantic and share some Greek love words, but I missed the boat and made a sandwich instead (my poor wife).

Love is hard. It is a difficult thing. I've started to warn young couples whom I do pre-marital counseling with not to fall prey to the dumb societal depiction of love. If I never watch another romantic comedy, it will be too soon. The plot is nearly always predictable, fake, and completely bogus. Some couple meets through a crazy series of events, and in forty-eight hours, they "love" each other (gag sound). No way! Love is hard.

Love is sleeping in a hospital beside a sick loved one, getting minimal sleep, and exerting self for their well-being. Love is sacrificing your wants because someone you love has a need greater than your wants. Love is having a consequence for your child when they do something wrong, even though it rips your heart out to watch them cry.

In the wedding ceremonies I perform, I've added the following line: "If you enter into marriage with selfishness, you shall gain nothing but pain. If you enter into marriage with selflessness, you will gain one of the greatest blessings from God." Many people enter marriage thinking of what they gain rather than what they will give. I think the truth behind the concept of genuine love is that it has a great cost.

John 3:16 is one of the most profound statements of love. "For God so loved the world that he gave..." Out of love came the greatest sacrifice that was or ever will be: Jesus, the Lamb of God. In many ways, the depth of our love can be measured by what we are willing to sacrifice.

When Jesus summarized the law by quoting the *Shema*, we sometimes wrongly perceive this as such a simple thing. I've heard sermons that say something to the effect, "All Jesus wants is you to simply love him and trust him." Yes. But let us not miss the depth of love. Love is hard. Love requires a giving of self, at least at some level. Jesus's summary of the law only affirms the writings of Paul in Romans, which tell us we are insufficient to satisfy the law. Without the love of Jesus, we didn't stand a chance.

At this point, I hope I've made the case for how difficult genuine love can be. If you are having trouble "loving your neighbor," I want to encourage your heart. We all fall short in love, but in Jesus, we find a love that is impossible without him. One of the things the Holy Spirit equips a follower of Jesus to do is to grow in our love of each other and God. We have divine help.

It is almost certain that we all have someone in our lives whom we may find difficult to love. Without the God of love, we cannot give the depth of love necessary to sustain some relationships. I encourage you to look at people thinking about how Jesus looks at you. Though you have faults, he loves you. Though you have said things, done things, and thought things that were not godly, God still loves you deeply. I encourage you to pray that God would help you see people with his grace.

Perhaps one of the most admirable moments in David's life was when he spared King Saul's life while Saul was hunting him. In 1 Samuel 24, Saul went into a cave to use the bathroom because the port-a-potties were all occupied. David was hiding in that very cave, and Saul's mission was to kill him. It was a prime opportunity for David to kill Saul and take the throne. However, David loved Saul. David knew he was God's anointed, and he spared Saul's life. David spared the man who had made his life miserable. David saw Saul as one God anointed and loved, and it gave him the ability to love him at the expense of selfish desire.

As we try to love others, we must do what David did. He saw Saul as God's anointed. He attempted to see people as God sees us through the lens of love and grace. Let us pray for God's help to see others as he sees us.

Reflection:

1. Are there people in your life right now that you find it difficult to love?
2. Are you looking at these people with grace and love?
3. Study 1 Samuel 24. What are some things David said and did when he saw King Saul in the cave?

CHAPTER THIRTEEN

A Standstill

So the work on the Temple of God in Jerusalem had stopped, and it remained at a standstill until the second year of the reign of King Darius of Persia.

— Ezra 4:24 (NLT)

Topic: God uses life's standstills as opportunities for growth.

For me, one of the most frustrating things in life is when you find yourself at a standstill. It is when you have done all you can do, and you hit a roadblock. At the time I'm writing this chapter, I'm building my kids a treehouse in the backyard. I love small (emphasis on small) building projects, but I often miscalculate materials. I'm finding myself at many standstills on the treehouse because I run out of screws, brackets, or boards.

In the book of Ezra, the scribe records that the work to rebuild the Temple of God had begun, but the people faced resistance from enemies. The enemies of Israel were desperately trying to stop the progress of the Jewish people. The Bible tells us these "enemies" hired builders who were deliberately sabotaging the work site. They encouraged local residents to "discourage and frighten the people of Judah to keep them from their work." (Ezra 4:4 NLT). Eventually, they even sent letters to the Persian king, falsely informing him that the Jews would become rebellious should they finish the temple. The result was that the king ordered the work be paused.

I imagine the frustration of the Jewish people was incredible. They had their plans, their calling right in front of them, but they couldn't step forward into it.

I have a friend, a pastor, who found himself in a painful situation, which led to a standstill. He was forcibly removed from his position at a church, and he and his family found themselves cast aside. I'm sure there were two sides to the story, but that didn't take away any of the pain.

Time passed, but he could not seem to find the next church God had for him. After a while, he became discouraged by the standstill.

The constant waiting and wandering carry a mental burden that is exhausting and disheartening. The standstills in life are the moments that test our persistence. Persistence is a great quality, and it is one that almost every successful person I know possesses. However, coupled with persistence must be the awareness to recognize God's part in the standstill.

The reality is that in the story in Ezra, the standstill had three culprits: the enemy, the ruler, and God. Yes.

That's right. God had a part in pausing the very work He ordained. We know this because God has sovereignty. He could have influenced the Persian king like he later did, but instead, he allowed the standstill.

Why does God allow standstills? I'm not sure we will ever know all the reasons, but I'm certain of one: we need the pause. Sometimes, God wants us to simply be still. In Psalm 46:10, the Bible says, "Be still and know that I am God." We spend so much time doing that we create an imbalance.

I notice the need for a standstill in most of my responsibilities, and perhaps one of the most frequent places I fail with this is in my role as a parent. Sometimes, we spend so much time filling the role that we forget to fill the person. Instead of overflowing the love of Jesus on our children, we can become tired and empty. Instead of our children seeing us as we want them to, they see an empty shell of who we want to be. While it may seem counterproductive, we need to sometimes ask God to help us face a standstill.

The Hebrew word *Shabbat* is where we get our very important word: Sabbath. The literal meaning of the word is "to cease." The term appears in every biblical section, with a total of 104 appearances in the

Old Testament.[6] I think we can conclude from this that God finds it important for us to simply stop. In God's moral law, written with his own finger (Exodus 31:18), he tells us to "Remember the Sabbath and keep it holy." God designated one day a week to stop our duties and reflect on him, to worship his goodness, greatness, and love.

Since God commanded us to stop, it should not be a surprise when sometimes he sends a standstill in our lives. Standstills are frustrating but important simultaneously. They teach us that the world will keep turning without us because God is in control, not us. He has simply given us some chores to do while we are in this life, but those chores are never meant to become more important than the one running the universe.

David wrote in Psalm 131:2, "But I have calmed and quieted my soul, like a weaned child with its mother; like a weaned child is my soul within me." Despite David's hardships, stress, and loss, he learned to have a calm and quiet soul. Is your soul calmed and quieted, or does your soul feel like it is in turmoil? The day-to-day life can quickly become a storm, but it is important that the soul feels calm despite what is happening outside. Sometimes, we feel an inner

---

[6] Bryan C. Babcock, "Sabbath," ed. John D. Barry et al., *The Lexham Bible Dictionary* (Bellingham, WA: Lexham Press, 2016).

restlessness or a weary soul. That is a key sign we need a standstill.

God is aware of what we need even when we aren't willing to admit it. Sometimes, God stops the movement. Sometimes, God pauses the progress. Productivity is not the absolute end goal. Remember that things holding the greatest value in this world are the scarcest.

What is God stopping in your life? Are you asking him to help you finish the task, or are you seeking his help, learning at a standstill?

Reflection:

1. Are you taking time each week to quiet your soul?
2. Do you feel like you are frustrated by the standstills in your life?
3. Have you considered that God is using the pauses?
4. What steps can you take right now to create times to reflect and rest in God's love and grace?

CHAPTER FOURTEEN
The Way of the Flesh

For the word of the LORD is upright, and all his work is done in faithfulness.

— Psalm 33:4

Topic: God's way is better than our way, even if it seems longer.

I once heard Dr. Charles Stanley preach a message about God's will. Dr. Stanley explained that God has a sovereign will (it will not be altered) and God has a permissive will. If you've ever asked the question: How can I live outside of the will of God? The answer is: God's love is so big he has room for your disobedience. God's permissive will is what allowed Adam and Eve to eat the fruit of the tree of knowledge of good and evil despite his command to abstain from that tree. Rather than force you to do exactly as you are commanded, God will allow you to wander and learn.

When I was a kid, I was in the Boy Scouts. We would go on frequent camping trips, but some of those stand out in my mind more clearly than others. I remember one trip well because of what happened. One evening, a group of us decided to leave the campsite and hike down to the lake to go fishing. It was a decent little hike, but it was less than a mile. While we were walking through the woods, we could see the lake through the trees in the distance. Then, some of us had a bright idea. We decided to get off the road and take a direct route to the water.

In our minds, heading directly to the water seemed to make sense. After all, the shortest distance between two points is a straight line (my geometry teacher would be proud). There were several things we did not consider, however. One of those was that the woods between the lake and the road were filled with dense brush and briars. Also, there was the potential to step on a yellow jacket nest, which one of us ended up doing.

By the time we got to the lake, we were all miserable. We were covered in scrapes and cuts from the briars. We had whelps from the yellow jacket stings, along with sore ankles and bruises. Fishing wasn't so appealing anymore, and we were all ready to just go home. Though the road was winding and longer than the direct route, it would have brought us to our destination in much better condition.

Sometimes I feel that my personal walk on God's path for me is similar. I often don't understand why God's way seems longer with unnecessary turns and twists. The shortcut, or direct route, looks much more appealing, but when I step off the trail God has set before me, I find all the nasty surprises he was keeping from me. There have been times in my life when I know, beyond a doubt, that if I had just listened to God's prompting, my road would have been much less painful.

Jesus told a story in Luke 15:11-32 that is one of the most famous stories in all of scripture. Charles Dickens is quoted as referencing the story as the "greatest short story ever written." It is the story of the prodigal son.

The Prodigal Son parable is filled with so many levels of theological truth and applications for life that a preacher could fill half of his year's sermons with a single text. I'm going to simply speak to one small piece of the story. It is the *way of the flesh.*

Jesus began the parable by telling us of two sons. The younger son decided he wanted to leave his father's house and see what the world had to offer. So, he asked his father for his inheritance in advance. The father, generous and loving, gave his son what he asked of him. So the son went his own way, only to find himself eating slop with pigs. The son, who was once a wealthy, well-dressed young man, finds himself now as a starving slave. In desperation, he began journeying back home to his father's home. His father was there to welcome him with open arms despite his foolish decisions.

The younger son's "flesh" made him believe there was something better out there away from his father. That same "flesh" or the physical aspect of humanity gives us the same lure today. The way of the flesh appeals to the human condition. It is self-seeking, impatient, greedy, and contrary to everything loving. Every time we choose the way of the flesh over God's way, we veer off of the best path, God's path, for our lives.

If you believe you have wandered off God's path for you, then do not be discouraged, but also do not be content. There is a better way for your life, but you are going to have to do something very few people are willing to do. You are going to have to turn around.

There is no equivalent word in Hebrew to match the English word "repentance." However, the concept is best illustrated by the word "return." The idea is to do an about-face and go the exact opposite way.[7]

Once, I was going to visit a terminally ill man and his family. The man lived outside of my town, and I was unfamiliar with the area. I relied completely upon my phone navigation. I looked at the map on my phone, and the little blue line did a giant circle, then came back to the guy's address. It was an eighteen-minute drive around this big loop, but on the little map, I could see a road that clearly went through the middle. I thought to myself, "Why in the world would it have me drive all the way around. Dumb thing! I can

---

[7] Brendan Kennedy, "Repentance," ed. John D. Barry et al., *The Lexham Bible Dictionary* (Bellingham, WA: Lexham Press, 2016).

just go that road and be there in no time." I decided to rebel against the phone's guidance.

I drove up to the turnoff, and I saw the dirt road that cut through the middle of the loop. I turned on the road and started driving. The phone navigation kept fussing at me, "Make a U-turn. Make a U-turn." Finally, I shut that thing up by stopping the directions. I kept driving, thinking that I was now the equivalent of Lewis, Clark, and Sacagawea.

As I came around a bend in the road, my confidence in my navigation skills quickly waned. I saw giant metal poles in the middle of the road. On the backside of those poles was tall grass, then a drop. I put the car in park and walked up to the roadblock. On the other side of the poles was a steep embankment (very steep) that led down to a wide creek. On the other side of the creek, I could see a house. I was pretty sure that was the home I was trying to reach, but without a good pair of boots, I wouldn't be crossing that creek.

There was only one thing to do: turn around. I had to swallow my pride and do a U-turn. Ironically, the "shortcut" added distance with every foot I drove from my route navigation. I was late to my appointment with the family, but there was a spiritual lesson to be gained. Sometimes, you must see that you are unable to reach where you want to be on the path you've chosen. You must turn around.

In Psalm 51, we read of David's heart of repentance. It is the snapshot of when David had to turn from his rebellion against God. He had to own his sin, and he had to ask for help. These are the words he wrote in Psalm 51:10, "Create in me a clean heart, O God, and renew a right spirit within me." David's writings bring to my mind a word that is always needed when we are heading in the wrong direction: change.

The idea of "turning around" is exactly what repentance is. It is a complete change in direction. In the story of the prodigal son, he walked right back up the road he had once chosen to walk in the opposite direction, away from his father. At the end of the parable, he chooses to return to his father and beg to be brought back as a servant, but his father awaits his return with open arms and celebration.

I believe this is true of our Father in Heaven today. He stands with open arms, wanting his children to turn around and come back to him.

It isn't too late to turn around. We need God's help to follow his path.

Reflection:

1.   Do you feel you are walking the path God has for you?
2.   If you don't feel you are on the right track, are you willing to change your direction?

CONCLUSION
Wind in the Sail

There is an old Irish blessing that says, "May the road rise up to meet you. May the wind be always at your back. May the sun shine warm upon your face, the rains fall soft upon your fields, and until we meet again, may God hold you in the palm of His hand." It is a beautiful way to part from old friends, and I share it with you, my friend.

I don't know where God is guiding you, but I pray you feel his helping hand. As you continue your journey, may you know that you are never alone. I pray you remember that just a small wind can move a large ship if you harness it. I pray you feel the wind in your sails and journey forward.

ABOUT THE AUTHOR

Carl Adam Wright was born in Lancaster, SC. He is married to Allison Wright, and they have two children: Lydia and Maxwell. He graduated from Anderson University with a Bachelors Degree in Christian Theology in 2010. Later, he completed his Master of Divinity degree at Southeastern Baptist Theological Seminary.

He has held various ministry positions since 2007, including roles as a Student Pastor, Associate Pastor, Church Planter, United States Army Chaplain, and Senior Pastor. Each opportunity has been filled with blessings, the privilege of meeting incredible people, and serving an awesome God.